The
Q&A
Guide to Understanding
YOUR HORSE

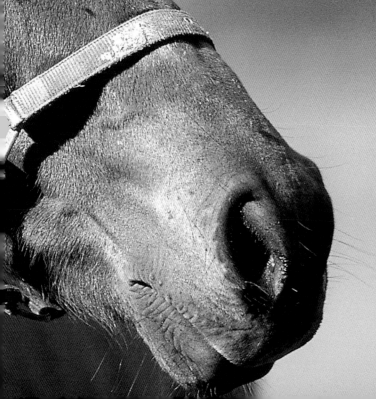

The
Q&A
Guide to Understanding
YOUR HORSE

MICHAEL PEACE & LESLEY BAYLEY

D&C
David and Charles

Contents

1 Think like your horse

Think Equus is Michael Peace's approach to handling and riding horses. It is not a set of structured techniques but a philosophy, a system of beliefs about how horses should be treated. The thinking and reasoning behind Think Equus have evolved over time, and hundreds of horses have given Mike's philosophy the thumbs up. From 'shut-down' dressage horses to wound-up racehorses, stallions in pain to innocent young horses, all have responded to Mike's unique and thoughtful approach.

The logic behind Think Equus and the application of it as a training tool were explained in the first book, *Think Like Your Horse*. This sequel takes a more in-depth look at the practical application of Think Equus, dealing with many of the common problems experienced by riders and handlers throughout the horse world.

Before examining specific problems we will look at the key elements which make up Think Equus and answer some of the most frequently asked questions.

THE FOUNDATION STONES OF THINK EQUUS ARE:

- Horse and rider/handler have their specific responsibilities and some shared responsibilities.
- In order for a partnership to work both horse and rider must give 100 per cent, and the relationship should be on a 50/50 basis with neither being the 'boss'. However, it is often necessary for the human half of the partnership to control the situations which horse and rider face. Both parties should work for the common good.
- Each party must show the other respect and courtesy. Each must pay attention to the other and be aware of each other's changing needs and motivations.
- Neither party should exploit the other's weaknesses or anxieties.
- Handlers and riders should be aware of the level and pace of the lesson so that their pupil (the horse) learns without undue stress or boredom. Each needs to pay attention to the other.

Q What responsibilities does a horse have?

In the natural world horses live in small herds, with each member co-operating for the good of all. Living in a herd provides a horse with security, friendship and the chance to reproduce.

The herd eats, sleeps and moves on together, with certain horses taking the decision to move the herd on. The animals will take turns at being on guard duty while the others sleep. If one horse senses danger he immediately alerts the rest of his herd. In order to survive the horse has two options: run, which is his preferred way of dealing with danger, or fight.

Basically, horses know how to survive and how to work together for the common good. They communicate with their own kind primarily through body language, and they also use their voices, for example a mare will call to her foal, and friends will greet each other with soft calls.

In the domesticated world life is very different for a horse. He may well be kept on his own and, even if kept with other horses, his time at liberty, just being a horse, is likely to be restricted. He will be expected to carry a rider and perform any number of activities, from hacking out to jumping across country, schooling to going into confined spaces – some of which then move. He will have his feet handled, objects put on his back, and he will be taken onto roads where cars will speed past. Horses have to learn to cope with all these things – they have to subdue their natural instincts and reactions and behave in a way that humans find acceptable.

Trainers who adopt the Think Equus approach will help their horses to find the solution so that they can live happily in our world. This may involve encouraging the horse to use the left side of his brain, the problem-solving, rational side, rather than just reacting instinctively.

Horses, like humans, have to learn to be responsible for their own actions. This is the only way in which they will learn. As an example, there is debate in the eventing world that horses are now trained to such a degree that they no longer have to think for themselves. Some people feel that this over-training can and has led to accidents; if a horse is not used to thinking for himself he probably cannot 'find a fifth leg' in a sticky moment when jumping and is likely to fall. However, a horse that has learnt to look after himself, for example when travelling over undulating terrain, or when working through a grid of jumps, will be able to extricate himself from tricky situations, often before the rider has even realised that anything is wrong. Just as humans learn most quickly from their own mistakes, so do horses.

IN A NUTSHELL

- Horses know how to co-operate for the common good.
- They are perfectly capable of being responsible for their own actions.
- They are capable of solving problems and subduing their natural actions.
- They are able to learn whatever we want to teach them – they can learn bad practices as easily as they learn good ones.

ADJUSTING TO A DIFFERENT WORLD

A horse has to learn to compromise in order to exist comfortably in our world. If he comes across people who understand horses and how they think, it will be easier for him to make the transition. If the horse has the misfortune to be 'trained' by someone who does not understand horses, the animal will find adjusting to life in the human world much more difficult. This is because his trainer is incapable of explaining to the horse in terms that he can understand how the horse should behave.

Sometimes the trainer does not even know how the horse should behave – for instance, the trainer who hangs on to a young horse's foot the first time the horse allows him to pick it up shows a basic lack of understanding of equine nature. A horse needs to be able to escape danger: for a horse to surrender his feet to a human takes a lot of trust. If the human then repays this trust by holding on to the foot the horse can only interpret this in one way: this human means to do me harm.

Q What are the rider or trainer's responsibilities?

Anyone who deals with horses should understand the nature of horses. Sadly, the fact that many horses start out as nice, genuine animals and end up being labelled dangerous or problem horses shows that too many people lack a real understanding of horses. The first thing any successful trainer needs to do is let go of his or her ego. With that out of the way we can all admit that the amount we really know about horses is pretty small – the great thing is that we have the opportunity to go on learning for the rest of our lives!

As the logical and problem-solving side of the human brain is used a great deal, we should, as trainers, be able to arrange situations to the benefit of both the horse and ourselves. We can set up the horse for success just by carefully choosing and presenting the lesson. This ability also extends to keeping the goal as a fluid target. Sometimes a horse will learn quickly, at other times he will need more help, perhaps to take a step back and consolidate one aspect before moving on. It is the trainer's responsibility to ensure that the learning process is enjoyable and progressive, stimulating but not overfacing.

Humans enjoy praise – so do horses. Most horses genuinely want to please – even those who have a negative attitude to life respond positively once they realise that a rider or handler is there to help them and is on their side. As trainers we should never forget the importance of telling our horse that he is good, that he has made the right choice. On the other hand, we do not need to tell a horse that he is wrong or bad by punishing him or by shouting at him. Humans do not like to be told they are wrong: most of the time you know you have made a mistake and it does not make you feel any better to have your errors pointed out. It is better to 'correct' your horse by showing him how to do the right thing and making it easy for him to get it right. Once he has succeeded then he can be praised. Horses respond to this kind of training – their usual response to being told off is to fight or withdraw into themselves, neither of which helps with the overall aim of producing a horse that is happy and willing to live alongside humans.

WHAT RESPONSIBILITIES ARE SHARED?

Both horse and rider have a responsibility to each other if a partnership is to work. If two people set up in business together, each with the same workload, but only one puts in any effort, the partnership is doomed to fail. The same applies to horse-and-rider combinations. Each has to make an effort – otherwise they may as well not bother at all.

Within the Think Equus philosophy it is important that horse and rider show each other courtesy as well as respect. This mare is pretty tough and has her own opinions on life, especially when it comes to walking through water. Mike is trying to show her a way of dealing with this, initially by simulating water with plastic on the ground. All the mare has to do is walk over it – but this is a big step for her and she needs time to think. When, as here, she is trying and thinking, Mike is courteous and leaves her alone to ponder

IN A NUTSHELL

- Humans need to let go of their ego.
- We need to make an effort to really understand the nature of horses.
- We set up the horse (and therefore ourselves) for success.
- We select and present lessons to the horse carefully to optimise the horse's success.
- We let the horse know we are there to help him.
- We make it easy for our horses to make the right choices and praise them for doing so.

Q Explain what you mean by a 50/50 partnership

Let Mike describe briefly how he came to develop the Think Equus philosophy:

'I knew nothing about horses when I started working with them at the age of 14, and this helped me to develop my own approach as I wasn't already indoctrinated by someone else's ideas.

'I was a jockey for a time and, by observing how the other lads dealt with horses, I began to see which approaches worked and which didn't. The riders who tried to bully their horses into behaving merely met their match in more ways than one and got into a battle. The riders who were more sympathetic had an easier life. They avoided battles, rarely pushed the horse to the point where he had to retaliate by bucking or rearing, and displayed all the basic principles of good horsemanship.

'Over time I realised that in order to make both my and my horses' lives easier I had to learn to empathise with them and see life from their point of view. Rather than get into a battle of wills each time a horse misbehaved I worked through each problem. If a horse was scared to go past something I was sympathetic. I'd say, "Okay, I understand why you're worried, but trust me and we'll get through it. It isn't a horse-eating monster, you are being irrational, so listen to me and we'll learn to deal with it together".

'I learnt to be sympathetic, but not so sympathetic that I didn't get the job done, and that approach led me to develop the 50/50 balance philosophy – teaching people to think like horses, and vice versa. That's you and your horse working in unison, without either party trying to control the other: a completely equal relationship.

'First I make the rules clear so the horse knows where he stands. Then I expect him to make an effort and co-operate. I meet him halfway, and then it is his job to do the same – which is where the balance comes in. I'm not going to do all the work while the horse goes to sleep; he has got to pay attention and put in an equal amount of effort. If the horse decides not to co-operate, I have every right to get after him and demand that he does.

'Horses are experts at communal living and they fully understand the concept of living in a co-operative group. If they were bargy in a herd situation, they would simply be barged back – that is the law of nature and one that every horse understands. I am merely mirroring a horse's natural behaviour by demanding that we work together in a small herd of two.

'An important point to consider when developing a healthy working relationship is that there is a difference between bullying a horse and meeting him halfway. To maintain a 50/50 balance it is essential that both sides make constant, minute changes to the relationship. Imagine balancing a

This pony is difficult to catch even in an enclosed area such as a school. Whatever the reason, the balance in the relationship is definitely out of kilter as the owner always has to make more effort than the pony in order to catch him. She often pursues him around the arena or field. In this partnership the pony definitely has the control

The second photograph shows the same pony at liberty in a field. Mike has not tried to catch the pony, but has proved to him that he will ignore rather than pursue him. Within a short while the pony was following Mike, and is now happy to be caught. The balance in the relationship has swung dramatically, with the pony relinquishing his position of power for a more balanced relationship

THE IMPORTANCE OF A BALANCED RELATIONSHIP

When working with horses the ideal is to have a 50/50 partnership, but the reality is usually different. However, we can still strive to get as close as possible to the 50/50 ideal. People often feel that they give their horses so much, in terms of time, money and commitment, yet the horse appears to give little back. Their horses may well feel the same! They may want more time at liberty, or more understanding riders, instead of the latest fashion in rugs or training gadgets!

pole vertically on the end of your finger. If you're good at balancing and have refined the art so that you are constantly making the tiny adjustments necessary to keep the pole in the air, then the whole process looks effortless. However, if you're not good at balancing you have to work harder because your adjustments are more erratic. That's how you should view the delicate balance in the relationship with your horse.

'The final point I would like to make is that horses do not hold grudges. They won't go off in a huff if we tick them off – that is human behaviour. If you give a horse very clear rules, it is up to him to co-operate and work with you. If he can't be bothered to make an effort, you are perfectly entitled to get after him. That's the language he understands and he will respect and deal with it just as he would with another horse.'

Much of the horse world operates on the basis that the human half of the combination has at least 51 per cent of the power, and often more. The Think Equus philosophy is that equal shares in a relationship results in a better whole as each party puts in 100 per cent commitment. Each party recognises the skills and benefits of the other, without resentment or fear, and as each party contributes their skills, the overall benefit to the partnership is one of continuing development. It's rather like a husband and wife who have a good relationship, working together so that they can

enjoy a better life. If one partner suddenly starts to contribute less then the balance of the relationship is altered, as there is more pressure on the other person. However, the relationship can soon be put on an even keel if the two people discuss the change and decide jointly how to progress towards a common goal.

It is vital that you understand how horses perceive events. This young horse is being mounted for the first time, and to date has been very wary of having a saddle on (as expected, his instincts have been very much to the fore). Traditional thinking and training often recommend that several people are involved at this crucial stage – one to hold the horse, one to give the rider a leg up, and the rider. From the horse's point of view this can be interpreted as the heavy mob! If a youngster is already rather sceptical, and then finds himself outnumbered, he is being set up to fight without actually having much say in the matter.

Here Mike prepares the horse for the actual step of being mounted by jumping up and down alongside the horse and then bellying over in front of the saddle. This still allows the horse the freedom to move, which is so vital for a prey animal

Q What do you mean by horse and rider showing each other respect?

Mutual respect is all about understanding a horse's power and not abusing yours. The best horsemen have an innate regard for the strength and power of a horse and are careful to remain respectful of this. Horses have the ability to do us a lot of harm if they choose to. Their reflexes are quicker, they are much, much stronger, and if they decide to kick out or squash us up against a wall there isn't a great deal we can do about it.

Luckily for us, horses rarely mean to do us harm – if they do it is only because of the treatment they have received at our hands, or because they are fearful of our actions and want to protect themselves. Horses are unaware of their size and strength in relation to us and they are fragile in this respect. It is our responsibility not to abuse this fragility or use it to bully the horse.

When people respect each other they are aware of each individual's feelings and personal space, and act accordingly. You would not start hurling abuse at someone without any provocation; you would not push someone around or try to intimidate them. If respect is lacking then these things can happen. It's like the gang of youths who walk down the street, not bothering to make way for other pedestrians. Such people will barge you out of the way with complete disregard for your well being. Occasionally such people are not aware that they are

Mike works with the mare, leading her, making changes of direction. Within a short while the horse's mindset is changing and she is paying him attention. Notice how her head is lowered and she is watchful of Mike, wondering where he will go next.

This rider has trouble with her horse under saddle, but as you can see, the root of the problem can be traced back to something much more simple – the horse's lack of attention and respect. The mare's eye is rolled away from her owner, showing that she is not paying attention and is not attempting to fulfil her half of the bargain

With her attention gained, Mike now works at making the mare more aware of his and her personal space. He turns, stops, moves off, and stops again. The mare soon learns to follow his every move, stopping a respectful distance behind him

being rude or ignorant, but often the underlying cause is simply that they do not show any respect for other people or their needs.

Sometimes horses are like this: those that will walk over the top of you, put their heads up in the air, or put their chests or shoulders towards you and come forward towards you without any regard for your safety. It may be that such a horse has not been taught to respect your space, or that he has been badly handled and has to get his aggressive act in before you have a chance to either be nice or aggressive.

Most horses are pretty nice, generous, sweet-natured animals. They already know how to be respectful – they have learnt from living in their herd how to approach older horses, how to behave and how to co-operate. Most young horses will approach human visitors to their field – if their inquisitive advances are met with whacks and shouting they will either not be so keen to meet humans next time, or learn to approach humans with a harder attitude, for example they may bite. The ignorant human handler will treat this development as proof that the horse is bad and will respond with more abuse, so creating a spiral of deteriorating behaviour.

The situation could have been so different – if a young horse's inquisitive advances overstep the mark then he can be respectfully put in his place using behaviour he will understand. As an example, a mare will discipline a pushy foal by shoving him away with her nose or exhibiting assertive behaviour. Humans can imitate this by pushing a horse's head away or stepping assertively towards them. The horse will understand this far more clearly than being shouted at or hit; he won't have any idea why this is happening.

The way in which a horse has been handled in the past affects his behaviour every day. If a horse is used to being hit by a handler then he may appear to be disrespectful; he may hold his head high in the air. A new owner can change this horse's attitude by showing him that he is not going to be hit, so there is no reason for the horse to have his head in the air.

If a horse is being genuinely disrespectful he may take a step towards you as if to shove you out of the way. You can quickly let him know that you are on to his game by backing him up. The technique is simple and effective.

A good rule is to treat your horse with the respect you would expect to receive yourself.

IT'S JUST COMMON SENSE...

If people respect each other, it's easier to get along and get things done. If horses and people respect each other more can be achieved. If respect is missing then it has to be re-established before any progress can be made. Horses can hurt people, and vice versa, but there is little to be gained if such situations develop.

Q How do you know a horse is showing you respect?

There are signs to look for – but bear in mind that you should not draw conclusions about a horse's state of mind from just one piece of evidence or behaviour. You should take a holistic approach. For instance, a person who is listening to you with their arms crossed may be defensive about whatever it is you are saying – or they may just be cold! In order to determine which you need to consider lots of other signals, and it's the same with horses. A horse that is being respectful has his head lowered, floppy ears, a softness in the eye and a relaxed body, and is probably licking and chewing. He will be following you with his eyes and ears whenever you are around him, not in a wary, fearful way, but in an interested, watchful one. He will be aware of where you are in relation to him at all times, and will step back politely to move out of your way.

Another sign of respect is when the horse yields to a request by you to move. He won't question you or put up a fight, but will accept your request and move politely away.

MAKE THINGS EASY FOR YOUR HORSE

Always make sure that the horse is capable of achieving everything you ask him to do. If you push him too hard or fail to make yourself understood the horse will start to lose faith in you. Instead, you should progress in small, easy stages so you can be genuinely pleased with a horse when he achieves something new.

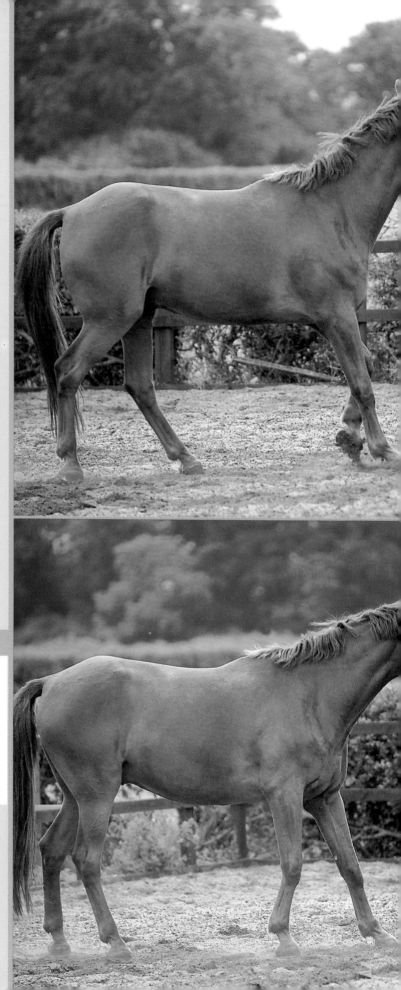

Right: If a horse encroaches on your space, back him away from you (top) and when he moves back – a mark of respect – show your appreciation by giving him a rub on the head

Q How can we show respect to a horse?

Have you ever had the experience of opening the door to someone and they have been so 'in your face' that you have had to take a step backwards? You would have felt that your space had been invaded and that the caller was not showing sufficient respect. Now apply that to your horse. Do you give the horse any time to adjust to your presence before you walk into his stable? Do you think your horse might feel as you did when you opened the door to the rude caller? You bet he does!

Think about how you move around your horse – try to make your body language more flowing so that you are less of a threat. This will let your horse know that you are working in a co-operative way rather than in a dominant way. Make your horse aware that you are about to do something rather than just going ahead and doing it! This can be achieved by your use of body language, and speed and direction of movement, rather than by using your voice. Your horse understands these physical factors because that is how horses communicate. In order to understand our verbal language we would have to teach him. In addition, the use of the voice is not a conclusive or consistent system – for instance, we don't say 'left' when we want our horse to turn left.

The secret of showing respect to a horse lies in never putting undue pressure on him, either emotionally or physically. It's important to appreciate what the horse is capable of and not pressure him to the point where he becomes upset or distressed.

Respect comes from empathising with a horse and understanding how his mind works. It's a case of working with him all the time to achieve that all-important 50/50 balance, rather than being domineering.

Don't forget that respect is something horses already understand. It is more a case of us having to understand respect. Mike feels that he really learnt the true meaning of mutual respect from working with horses that had hurt people in the past. He had to communicate to these horses that he was respectful of them and was not going to abuse them. 'My mental fitness was hugely important,' explained Mike. 'It's the key to leadership. If any of these horses had suspected that I had the slightest doubt about handling them they would have exploited the situation if they were that way inclined. If a horse is looking for help and he senses doubt in me then he will know that I cannot help him. Therefore keeping any doubts at bay is vital. Improving your mental fitness is something that is done incrementally, just as you develop other skills.'

TIPS FOR SUCCESS

- Make sure you keep some saliva in your mouth.
- Take deep breaths to keep a good supply of oxygen going round your body.
- Wear clothes that make you feel comfortable and protected, for example two or three layers if dealing with a horse that bites, a hard hat and decent boots.

Q How can you let a horse know that you are on his side?

The most important point to consider is how you build the horse's confidence and put him in a situation where he cannot do anything wrong. This is especially pertinent if the horse you are dealing with is sensitive. In the past the horse may have tried and failed and been told off – he is probably now reluctant to try. Trainers who adopt the Think Equus approach would feel it was their job to show such a horse that it's OK to try, and that he can do so without worrying about getting things wrong. Get your horse to do something and then tell him how good he is. Horses, children and adults all like to be praised. They will all be more likely to try harder and to do more if they are rewarded. If horses or people are constantly criticised for getting things wrong they stop trying because it is too painful for them.

We want our horses to try and we have to reward them for their efforts – what seems like a tiny try may in fact be a big shift in thinking for a horse.

So always set things up for a horse in such a way that you give him every chance to succeed. Then, when he does succeed, show him that you are pleased with the outcome. Horses are hugely sociable animals, so a genuine rub on the head is enough to let the horse know he has done well. He will appreciate this and feel good about himself.

For example, if you are teaching a young horse to be well behaved in traffic, set the situation up to make it as easy as possible for him to cope with the challenge. Choose a quiet country lane with wide verges for your first few rides. Then, every time he manages to tolerate a car coming past, let him know how pleased you are with him.

If you headed out onto a busy road instead, the horse would become upset, you would have nothing to praise him for, and the situation would turn into a negative one. The horse would soon start to associate traffic with unpleasant behaviour and that's often how problems and phobias start.

It's important to show your horse respect, and you can also let him know you're on his side by taking care of little details such as making him comfortable when you tack up by getting the forelock out from under the browband and ensuring the girth is not too tight.

To work successfully with horses they have to know that you are on their side. This means being aware of how the horse perceives you. For instance, Mike has crouched down so that this foal won't feel threatened by a potential predator. The foal has no reason to fear Mike now, and his natural curiosity will take over

Q When would either horse or rider be in a position to exploit the other's weaknesses or fears?

People tend to be competitive and will take advantage if some-one shows any weaknesses – this happens in business situations at all levels every day. You can probably think of instances in your own offices. As people often want to be the best they can fall into the trap of letting the achievement of goals override common sense or decency. Consequently some horses will be pushed beyond their mental, physical or emo-tional limits by riders determined to compete and succeed at any cost. Mike has realised that many young talented horses find their way to him because someone has pushed them too far, too quickly, and the horse is reacting by behaving badly. Instead of patiently nurturing their talent, the owners of these horses have been swept along in search of even greater success without thinking about the impact of accelerated learning and training on their horse's young body and mind.

It is all too easy for a human to exploit a horse, especially as most horses are genuine types who try their hardest until they reach a point when they have nothing more to give.

Horses can easily exploit people as well – we all know of owners whose horses show them no respect, will not be led, tied up, stand when mounted and so on. Such horses have realised that they can take charge and have done so.

Generally speaking, when either party exploits the other, the relationship is not particularly enjoyable for either horse or rider. A rider may have to be continually or even increasingly brutal in order to keep his horse in order, or he may find that his dominated horse loses the sparkle, willingness or freedom of movement which initially made his dressage or jumping per-formances so memorable. A horse that is constantly exploiting his rider's fears and being difficult to handle usually starts to behave when shown an easier way to live.

The way to avoid such conflicts is to work within an area of tolerance known as the 'middle ground'. The Think Equus prin-ciple is that working within this area of tolerance means that either horse or rider can make a mistake without feeling the need to exploit or resent the other and without permanent damage to the relationship.

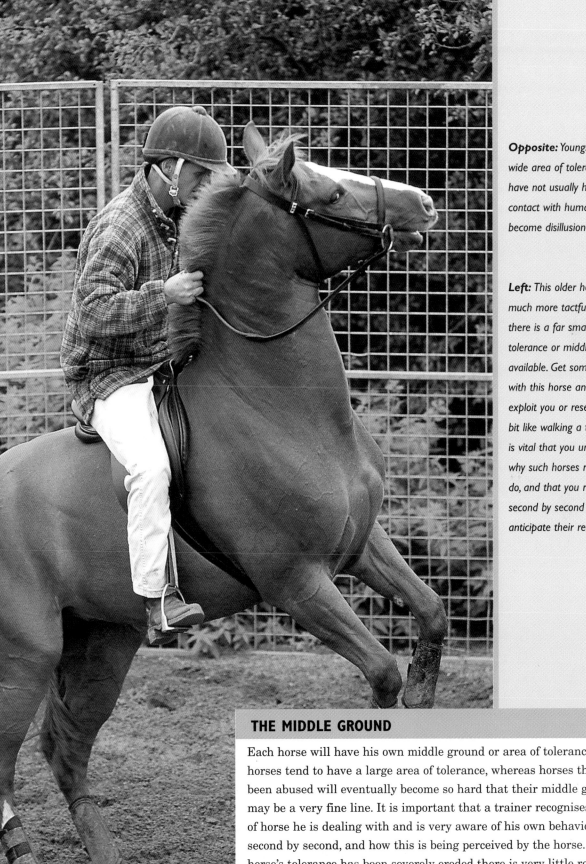

Opposite: Youngsters have a wide area of tolerance as they have not usually had sufficient contact with humans to become disillusioned

Left: This older horse requires much more tactful handling; there is a far smaller area of tolerance or middle ground available. Get something wrong with this horse and she'll exploit you or resent you: it's a bit like walking a tightrope. It is vital that you understand why such horses react as they do, and that you read them second by second in order to anticipate their reactions

THE MIDDLE GROUND

Each horse will have his own middle ground or area of tolerance – young horses tend to have a large area of tolerance, whereas horses that have been abused will eventually become so hard that their middle ground may be a very fine line. It is important that a trainer recognises the type of horse he is dealing with and is very aware of his own behaviour, second by second, and how this is being perceived by the horse. If a horse's tolerance has been severely eroded there is very little room for error and the trainer needs to be someone who truly understands this.

Q Is there ever justification for hitting a horse?

If you are talking about beating or punishing a horse, then no, there is never any justification for this. If you need to shove or bump a horse in order to equalise the balance of the relationship however, then yes, this could be justified – but only if it is for the right reasons, not out of temper.

There is no place for brutalising a horse, but there is a need to correct the horse occasionally in order to maintain a 50/50 balance. If you use no more force than one horse would to another in a herd situation, then that is acceptable to him. That is the law of nature and he will respect it. If you brutalise a horse or sting him with a whip, however, that is not acceptable and you will lose his respect.

Q How do I get my horse's attention?

To get a horse's attention you need to be a good teacher. It's all about being clever enough to gain a horse's attention without having to resort to shock tactics. If a schoolteacher bangs a book down on a table he may have everyone's attention for a few seconds, but it is the wrong kind of attention. His pupils are not listening to him because they want to, but because he has forced them.

A really good teacher will be cleverer than that. Think back to your school days and your favourite teachers. Often you can't quite pinpoint the reason why they were so effective, but they had that certain something that made you want to listen. That's what you have got to achieve with your horse.

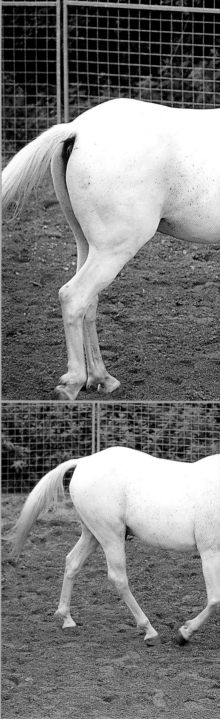

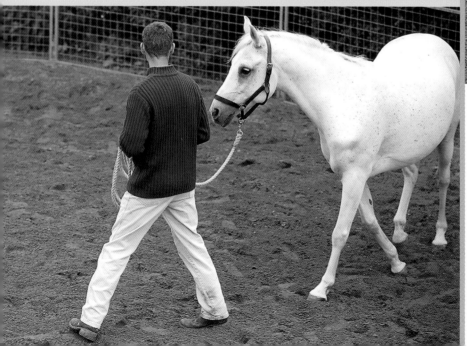

Left: This horse is being taken through the leading exercise and has started to pay attention to Mike's movements

Top: Then the horse becomes distracted. This can easily happen, but there is no point in shouting at the horse or jerking wildly on the lead rope. Instead the horse has to be carefully reminded about the job in

hand, so Mike gently draws the horse's head round to him

Above: *Having been shown what is expected, the horse directs his attention towards Mike again. The horse had made a mistake but was given the chance to put it right. All this has been achieved without either horse or rider becoming stressed*

You've got to find the right balance between gaining your horse's attention and respect, and not spoiling it by pushing him too hard or being too easy on him. It is a delicate balance and it takes practice, so watch other people who you consider to be good teachers and see which techniques they use. Try to keep each lesson as interesting as possible for the horse, and up the pace to keep the session rolling.

GETTING YOUR HORSE'S ATTENTION

Have your horse in a normal headcollar with an extra-long lead rope if possible. There is no need to use stronger headcollars such as pressure halters. The whole point is that horse and handler should show each other mutual respect and attention. This is not feasible if you are using a pressure halter that can, in the wrong hands, cause considerable discomfort and even pain.

Set yourself and your horse up for success by initially working in an area/environment where your horse cannot be distracted. Use your horse's stable and start by asking him politely to take a step towards you, rewarding him with a rub on the head when he does. Then move to his other side, ask for a step towards you and reward him. He will soon learn that coming towards you when asked is a nice thing as he is made to feel good.

If your horse is not stepping towards you check your position – are you standing in his way and blocking his movement? Build stops and changes of direction into the exercise – if your horse is paying attention he will be following your every move, with his head lowered, his eye soft, and his whole body relaxed.

How do you know when a horse's attention is wandering, and what can I do to stop it?

If a horse's mind is beginning to wander he will stop watching what you are doing and stare at something more interesting instead. He may barge into you if you are leading him, or stumble into your personal space. If you are riding, the horse may snatch the reins out of your hand or trip up because he is not looking where he is going.

If you are in a busy environment such as a show and there is plenty going on to distract the horse, you have to make yourself more interesting than the surroundings. You need to up the pace of the lesson and keep everything moving. If you are in the saddle, make lots of changes of direction and pace to bring the horse's attention back to you.

If the horse gets distracted while you are leading him, draw his head towards you to get him focusing, correct the horse each time he pushes into your space and try gently nudging his head from side to side to relax him.

Always remember the 50/50 balance. Your horse must put an equal amount of effort into the relationship, so expect him to listen and work with you all the time.

To keep a horse's attention you need to keep the horse moving and stimulated – some horses are so laid-back that when working to get their attention you have to do things faster than you would normally. You have to work at a level that is suitable for that particular horse and observe your horse's reactions second by second so that you can adjust the pace of the lesson accordingly. If your horse's attention wanders it is important to just draw his attention back to you with a firm but not jerking feel on the lead rope. Remember that you want to make it easy for him to do the right thing, and that there should be mutual respect and courtesy. Watch out for yawning as this indicates mental tiredness; you should stop the lesson before the horse gets to a point where he cannot give you any more. You need to be very aware of how your horse is thinking and perceiving and how he may react. It is worth putting yourself into your horse's skin and so view your proposed lesson through his eyes, before you even start the lesson.

DON'T OVERDO YOUR TRAINING SESSIONS

Horses, like humans, have different concentration spans. Young horses, like young children, find it hard work to concentrate for anything more than very short periods of time. So you need to get your horse's attention, work on the lesson you need to teach him and finish before his mind has wandered. His attention span can be extended as his training progresses but it is up to you to help him, recognising when he is tiring and so finishing the lesson early if necessary. Young horses in particular will find their training mentally tiring.

Q How do you manipulate a horse's space and movement?

Horses understand how to manipulate space and movement for their own benefit – they learn these skills in the herd environment and you can see this happening all the time in groups of horses. A more dominant horse will move another horse away from the water trough, a mare will manoeuvre her foal so that she can protect it from unwanted attention, a horse will encourage his friend to indulge in mutual grooming, and so on. Horses achieve all this through their body language, and we need to know how to imitate this and use it.

Adopting an aggressive stance – drawing yourself up to your full height, squaring your shoulders, holding the arms out to the side and maintaining eye contact with a horse – will move him away from you. However, you can be much subtler; horses themselves are subtle creatures and recognise the slightest change in another horse's, or a human's, body.

Horses will recognise your importance (or indeed your insignificance) in their environment by your ability to manipulate their space and movement. You do this by getting your horse to step towards you and move around when you ask for respect and attention. You teach a horse to respect your space by backing him out of your space if he oversteps the mark. This is all telling your horse that you are important as you can control his movements. This can be applied in other situations such as loading.

Once you are aware of space and movement you can also stop a horse manipulating you. It is not uncommon for people to have problems mounting their horses. Often this is because the horse has learnt that by shifting position a little he can have his owner moving all over the place, trying to get on, failing, moving the mounting block to where the horse is now standing, trying and failing again. In these situations the horse is, with very little effort, making the owner move a great deal, and without any benefit to the owner. The way round the problem is to stop the horse manipulating you. You stay still and the horse has to move around you so he is expending more energy than you are. He will soon realise that moving is not giving him any benefit and will stand to be mounted.

Horses learn about manipulating space and movement from the minute they are born. The mare moves her foal around using her body language. This educational process is continued within the herd. You can see here how the horse is manipulating the rider's movement so that the rider has to constantly move and shift position as she attempts to mount. The horse will be happy to do this all day: he is expending very little energy for a great deal of benefit. To solve this mounting problem the roles have to be reversed!

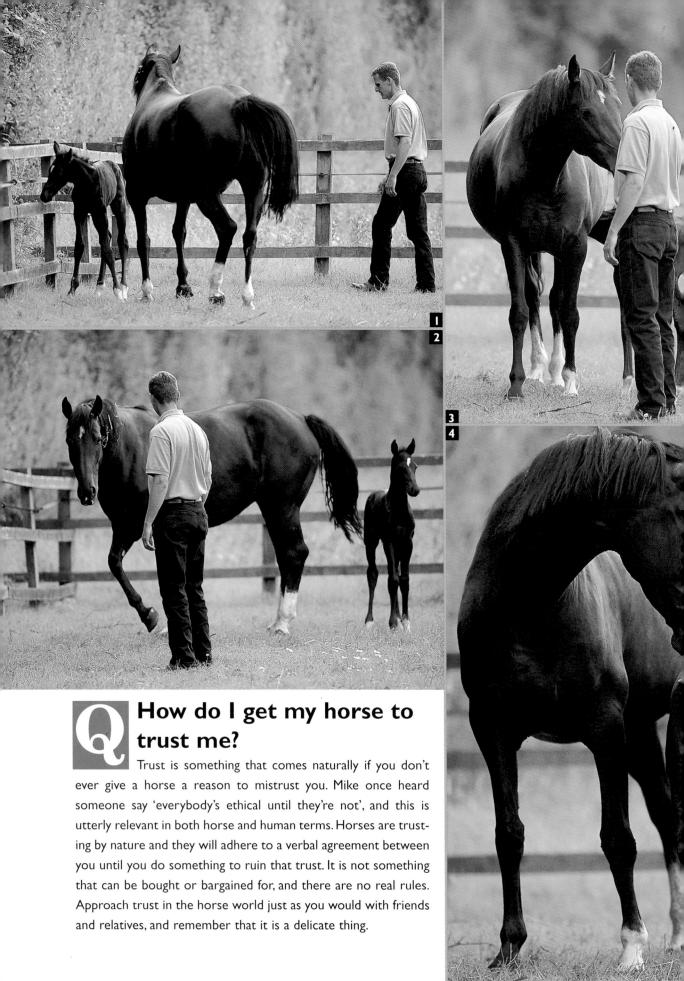

1
2
3
4

Q How do I get my horse to trust me?

Trust is something that comes naturally if you don't ever give a horse a reason to mistrust you. Mike once heard someone say 'everybody's ethical until they're not', and this is utterly relevant in both horse and human terms. Horses are trusting by nature and they will adhere to a verbal agreement between you until you do something to ruin that trust. It is not something that can be bought or bargained for, and there are no real rules. Approach trust in the horse world just as you would with friends and relatives, and remember that it is a delicate thing.

1 A mare's response to human contact will have an effect upon her foal's attitude to people. This mare has never met Mike before and is naturally protective of her foal, placing herself between them

2 To reassure the mare that he means no ill, Mike keeps his body language non-aggressive and quietly allows the mare to check him over

3 The mare has accepted Mike's presence and both she and her foal are relaxed

4 The trust is such that the mare is happy for Mike to make contact with the foal as he suckles. Taking his lead from his dam, the foal is totally relaxed about this human contact

Q Taking all the elements of Think Equus, what are the key things to remember when handling horses?

- Clarity – you must be quite clear in your own mind about how horses think and how they perceive the world. You also need to understand how the horse reads and perceives your every action, thought and emotion. You must also put away any doubts – your horse needs to know that you know where you're going.

- Consistency – horses respond to consistent, fair, firm handling. They will be confused if one day you are impatient and harsh with them and the next day you are too soft. You must work in the centre of the middle ground. You must also let go of your ego. It is important to put away any negative feelings you have about the horse. If you can remain detached and unemotional it is easier to get the job done.

- Work second by second – don't get too hung up on goals. Be aware of your horse the whole time, work with him and respond to him in this timeframe. Finish at any point – and always at a good point. Under this philosophy a bad situation should not have been allowed to develop because you are working second by second, picking things up, anticipating and setting the horse up for success.

- Partnership – you and your horse are in this together. You both need to put in the effort and commitment.

Remember that horses do not like to be anxious or aggressive – they just want to get on with life each day as easily as they can. Horses are usually relieved when they realise that you are on their side and just want to help them.

Horses, whether young, old, problem animals or not, all want a trouble-free life. They have simple needs and dislike complications. If you can show a horse you can genuinely help him, he will gladly take you up on your offer

The youngster must learn to respect your personal space – barging is unacceptable in both the horse and human world

FINN: THE JUVENILE DELINQUENT

It's fair to say that 18-month-old bay gelding, Finn, came into the world armed with enough attitude to fill the Grand Hall at Olympia. The cheeky youngster was literally born a fighter and showed his mum little respect from the word go. He saw the poor mare merely as a supplier of milk as opposed to a guiding light, and by the time he was weaned she seemed glad of the rest.

Bred by horse-loving sisters Maureen and Gillian, Finn was a force to be reckoned with, the likes of which they had never seen before. 'Finn's mum, Fair Artist, is 26 and had bred four gorgeous, sweet-natured foals before Finn, so we presumed he would be of the same ilk,' says Maureen. 'Instead out came this little horse who was a devil to handle, even when he was a tiny foal.

'We had to have him gelded at four months old as he kept rearing up at us and striking out with his feet. When the vet came to trim his feet Finn leaned right back on the rope and squealed his head off. We thought, "We've got a right one here!"'

Time for action

Maureen and Gillian had experience of Mike's approach to horsemanship with other youngsters he'd trained for them and were keen for him to meet Finn. By this time, Finn was a boisterous youngster and the sisters were at a loss as to how to handle him. He reared up at them, barged them out of the way, kicked out and often bit.

'He was a complete hooligan,' says Mike. 'You may expect to see this type of behaviour in a horse who is afraid and perhaps fighting for his life. In Finn's case it was almost as though he was doing it for fun. He was like a youth that gets pleasure out of smashing up phone booths! He had a very extreme character and displayed the kind of behaviour I have only ever seen before in bottle-reared youngsters. Bottle-fed foals have a tendency to become humanised if handled incorrectly and often realise their own strength, have no fear and start pushing people around. Finn was a horse who displayed just this kind of cocky over-confidence, yet it seemed he'd had a perfectly normal upbringing.'

At the age of 10 months Finn, who's an Irish Draught x Thoroughbred, went to spend a week at Mike's yard. Getting him there, however, was quite another story. First, Maureen and Gillian couldn't catch him; then, once they had managed to grab hold of the juvenile delinquent, he refused to go in the lorry.

'Because of his general disregard of people it was initially quite hard to gain enough of Finn's attention to get him loading into the lorry,' says Mike. 'Finn wouldn't listen to me or even try to set foot on the ramp. He wasn't scared; he just wasn't having any of it.

'Eventually he decided to listen and then walked into the lorry. Strangely, when I got him to my stables, he wouldn't unload! It would be quite easy to get annoyed with a horse like Finn but it wouldn't help things so, as it was lunchtime, I decided to take his headcollar off and leave the ramp down. I closed the yard gates and went for lunch. An hour later when I returned he'd unloaded himself and was happily grazing outside the lorry.'

Mike's Solution: It was evident that Mike was going to have his work cut out getting this feisty little chap to co-operate. 'His tendency was to be very aggressive and attempt to fight his way out of every situation he found himself in,' says Mike. 'Normally you can expect to find this behaviour in horses who have been mistreated somewhere along the line, but I knew Gill and Maureen, and Finn had had the best of care right from when he was born. It seemed it was just in his nature to behave this way.

'At first Finn simply saw me as someone else to push around. In a herd situation he'd never get away with it and my job was to show him how he should behave to fit in.

'My Think Equus approach to life is based on having balance in every relationship with the emphasis on collaboration, not dominance. Finn seemed to think he had to be in control and his negative behaviour was throwing everything out of balance. He needed to realise that he wouldn't have a future if it continued the way it was. We had to meet halfway or it wouldn't work.

'Before long Finn tried to push and bite me to gain some of my space and take control of me. I had to show him in no uncertain terms where his space ended and my space began. He needed to realise the definite line dividing where he existed and I existed. It's a simple rule – we have our own space, and can enter each other's space, provided we are polite, but pushing and biting is impolite behaviour in the horse world and in the human world too. In the horse's world impoliteness will be met with impoliteness. Finn soon learnt that it was easier to be a bit more considerate. It didn't take him long to get the message that life was so much easier if he was a bit more thoughtful and polite. We did leading work in walk and in trot with lots of changes of direction to get him listening and a bit sharper with his responses. If he lapsed into his old ways I backed him up, getting him out of my space, and back to where he could exist without trouble. Then I'd reinforce this by giving him a rub on the neck to prove the point before continuing with the lesson.

'The key thing is not to be aggressive, but just assertive enough to make the point without escalating the situation and getting into a confrontation. Just like a boisterous child, Finn is intelligent and curious and likes having things to focus on, something to grab his attention.'

Back home again

By the end of the week Finn's behaviour was much improved, and Mike accompanied him home. 'Finn was transformed and so much better to handle when he came back from Mike's,' says Gillian. 'He was 100 per cent improved. He was more polite and Mike gave us lots of tips on how to work with him.

'Mike explained the importance of keeping the relationship 50/50 and not letting Finn get the upper hand, but not bullying him either. Seeing what Mike had achieved gave us a lot of confidence and actually made perfect sense. It was a relief to know that Finn could be handled well and wasn't a complete monster.'

Finn's improved behaviour has continued and Mike reckons he will really enjoy being broken in and ridden when the time comes. 'He has a very active mind and at the moment he's just trying to find ways to fill his days,' says Mike. 'Once he is being worked that will give him a whole lot more to think about and concentrate on, so it will be a positive challenge.'

Gillian and Maureen have plans to start long-reining Finn once he has turned two, and are pleased that Mike has managed to turn their unruly baby into a promising young horse.

Finn still finds ways to break up his day: 'We moved him to a paddock near a sports field and Finn soon became an avid football fan,' says Maureen. 'He was fascinated by the players and learned that if he stood by the goal post, the ball would often come over the hedge and land in his field. He would then amuse himself by chasing the goalie back out of the field when he came to retrieve the ball. On one occasion he chased one of the players twice round a six-acre field. The guy had to have a lie down before resuming play.'

2 Less-than-perfect horses and riders

If you look through the 'Horses for Sale' columns in magazines and newspapers you could be forgiven for thinking that some people own perfect horses: descriptions such as 'excellent to catch', 'suitable for almost any rider', 'bombproof' and 'superb paces' are common. Why is it that if one then goes to see these so-called paragons they often fail to meet up to expectations? It is partly down to the fact that some owners do view their horses through rose-tinted glasses, while other people will swear black is white in order to off load the horse they can no longer afford or that has scared them witless. It is also true that the perfect horse does not exist – and that what one rider would regard as their ideal horse would be someone else's nightmare!

From the horses' point of view, less-than-perfect owners and riders also exist! Perhaps someone is hot-tempered and likely to vent their anger on their horse, or is too heavy for their horse, or does not know how to keep their horse properly. People and horses are less than perfect for a whole multitude of reasons.

However, in reality most of us are doing our best to get along as well as we can. Horses generally try their best to please, and people generally try to understand and help their horses. All this is made much easier if we can admit to our own and our horses' strengths and weaknesses and use this knowledge to positive effect.

But human nature being what it is, it is difficult for most people to take a long, hard look at themselves and honestly say what's good or bad. If someone suffers from low self-esteem they can easily come up with their bad points but are unable to recognise their strengths. On the other hand, the extremely self-confident person may not like to admit to their weaknesses.

The point of this chapter is to enable you to recognise good and bad points in both yourself and your horse, and to show how these can be handled in order for both of you to progress.

Q What qualities do you think a rider should possess?

These could include riding skills such as a secure jumping position, a good dressage position, the ability to see a stride, to remain in balance with the horse, and to get the most out of any horse. Other skills such as positive thinking and keeping focused under pressure could also be included.

Some people would place more emphasis on an understanding of the horse and an empathy with the animal than on actual riding ability. Others would not even consider this.

Everyone's idea of a rider's qualities will vary according to their own perception of a rider's job and their own experiences of the world. Ambitions for the future will also affect how we view things. If winning competitions is a major motivating factor we will be travelling along a different road than someone who rides purely for the pleasure of being out in the countryside.

QUALITIES TO STRIVE FOR

Accepting that we are all looking at the world through different eyes, there are some qualities we should all strive for in order to make life better for both horse and rider. These are:

- An understanding of the horse's nature. Think like your horse and you will be able to train him much more successfully to cope with the ups and downs of everyday life.
- An independent seat. We have to work hard to achieve this as most of us are not natural riders. It is human nature to grip with our legs and hang on via the reins, but this behaviour sets off alarm bells in the horse and tells him to get rid of the danger on his back.
- An open, questioning mind. Many people are taught to ride but are not encouraged to think for themselves or to ask questions. Some people like this because it saves them the effort of thinking, but they end up riding in a rather mechanical way, doing the same thing over and over, irrespective of how the horse reacts. It is much harder to think about what you are being asked to do, work out whether it makes sense to the horse, think about whether you can make things better or clearer for him, and so on. However, the quickest way to progress is to challenge, to question, to think, to try something, review the result, and seek out ways to improve.
- A willingness to keep going when everything seems set against you. No one finds horsemanship easy, and there will be countless occasions when you wonder why on earth you spend so much time and money on horses. Every top rider has come close to the brink and almost given up – but then something drove them on. If you want to achieve success with horses you have to work hard – there's no way round it!

Bearing all this in mind, you should realise that whatever your current level of ability with horses you can improve. Take the four qualities above – the fact that you are reading this book means that you are already working on point one!

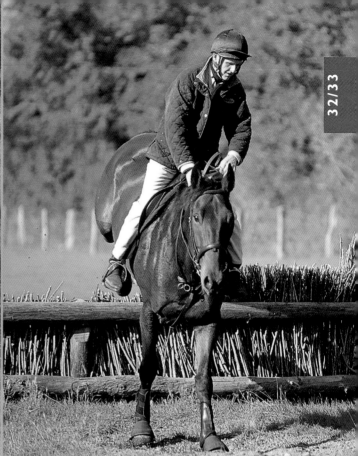

Above: *It is difficult to stand back and assess your own riding or work out a solution to a problem. Sometimes you can unwittingly create problems for yourself just by trying too hard. This horse and rider are attacking this fence. This may be keenness or anxiety on the part of either one or both of them. You may be able to recognise that this is a problem for you, but the question is: how do you deal with it?*

The second photograph shows the same horse being jumped by Mike just a few minutes later. The horse has slowed himself up considerably because Mike has a very light contact on the horse's mouth so there is no chance of a pulling match being initiated. Now the horse's usual rider can see that the horse is perfectly capable of jumping the fence without her having to work so hard. She tried this method herself with equal success

Left: *Take the opportunity to learn from studying photographs of yourself. You can see that this rider tends to take his weight on his knees and that he has no strength in his lower leg position. He has recognised this and is now working hard to improve it*

Q So how do I make a realistic assessment of myself?

■ As far as riding ability goes, you can ask a trusted and experienced instructor for advice. A good instructor should give you constructive feedback so that you are motivated to improve – after each lesson ask for some homework exercises, and make sure you do them!

■ Have your lessons or competitions captured on video – again, ask your instructor for feedback. If you do not have an instructor, get a friend to comment on your good points, and to highlight areas where you can improve. Note that we use the phrase 'areas of improvement' rather than 'bad points'! The language you use when talking about or to yourself affects your self-perception. Many people need to raise their self-esteem, and using positive language, focusing on achievements rather than failures, helps enormously.

■ Think about the kind of rider you want to be. Do you have a role model? If you pick Blyth Tait, for example, work out what it is that you admire about Blyth's riding. If it is his cross-country panache, how can you work towards achieving that? Do you need to invest time in gridwork to improve your balance and co-ordination? Would some sports psychology sessions help with your confidence when riding across country? Think laterally and consider all options. For instance, put yourself in the position of your instructor – what would they say about your current ability when riding across country?

■ Apply the Think Equus philosophy to your own training. Break down any problem into small, achievable chunks: for example, what are the rider qualities required in riding well across country?

  ■ Being able to stay in balance with a horse as he crosses various terrain.

  ■ Being able to present a horse to a jump successfully.

  ■ Being able to control the horse's pace and direction.

  ■ Being able to get the horse fit enough to deal with the demands, and so on.

Once you have worked out the various areas the overall task will seem less daunting, and you can reward yourself for smaller achievements en route.

■ Develop an eye for good and bad riding. If you want to ride well across country, for example, watch videos of riders at Badminton and Burghley. Look carefully at how they ride in between fences, up to and over fences, and when riding away from the fences.

Watch how the horses react. Notice how some riders are much more skilled at making the job easier for their horse.

- Watch people at the lower levels of eventing, dressage and show jumping. Examine their horses and start to appreciate whether the horses are relaxed, happy, worried, being put under too much pressure, and so on.

- Apply your critical eye to watching yourself riding on video. Try to detach yourself, as if you are watching another rider. How could this rider improve her position to get another few marks in a dressage test? What exercise could she use to get her horse more obedient? What one thing could this rider do to make the overall picture look more harmonious? How could she put more 'oomph' into the canter? (Notice how the questions are phrased to elicit solutions or positive comments rather than just negative feedback.)

IN A NUTSHELL

As there is always so much more to learn about riding and horse care it should be easy enough for us to identify some areas for improvement. Just as we want to make doing the right thing easy for our horse, so we can apply this method to our own progress:

- Decide on the goal and break it down into achievable chunks.
- Get help from the right people.
- If something is not working, change what you are doing – for example, this might mean changing instructors.
- Reward yourself for your progress so that you maintain the motivation to succeed.

Top: *If you want to assess your riding make use of videos and photographs. Watch out for your particular habits: for example, do you always give the outside rein away, as shown here?*

Left: *Use positive images (this photo, for example, shows an example of a good outside rein) as reminders of your qualities. Be aware of your weaknesses but do not focus on them – concentrate instead on your good points*

Q How does conformation affect a horse's purpose in life?

Conformation is how the horse is put together – the better his shape the more likely he is to lead a useful life without falling prey to soundness problems. When looking at a horse's conformation the overall picture should be pleasing – if there is something which really strikes you, this could be a problem area. For instance, a horse may have a very large head compared to the rest of his body, or he may have an unusually long back. Anything which detracts from an overall impression of balance and symmetry may lead to problems in the long term.

We'll take a brief look at some of the ideals, but the best way for you to learn about conformation is to go out and look at horses. Look at the ones that are consistently successful in their chosen disciplines, taking into account not just their good points but also their defects and their characters. Conformation plays an important part in a horse's success, but so does training, and perhaps, most important of all, so does the horse's heart: his generosity. Some animals overcome all kinds of problems and become winners because they have 'big hearts'.

When assessing conformation you need to consider the horse's age, as this may explain some of your findings – for instance, older horses may have dipped backs and their legs may show more signs of wear and tear

Opposite:
1 This mare is well proportioned, but since she has not been worked recently there is a lack of muscle development
2 Toes turned either in or out will result in excessive strain being placed upon the limbs
3 The hoof/pastern angle in the forefeet, and the angle of the shoulder, should be the same at around 45 degrees to the horizontal
4 This horse is pigeon toed, and now has degenerative bone disease in the knee as a result of the limb receiving uneven concussive forces
5 This horse is over at the knee and has very big joints

AN EYE FOR A HORSE

Some lucky people seem to possess this naturally, and can recognise a well put-together animal even if he's fat, hairy, covered in mud and standing several yards away! But the vast majority of people have to work hard to appreciate conformation and to gain the necessary experience to become a good judge of horses.

This horse's roach back is the first thing that strikes you. But you must always watch a horse move, as this horse had very nice paces. The muscles around his back were very tense, but soon softened once he was ridden using the Think Equus approach

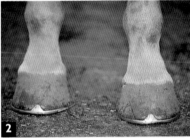

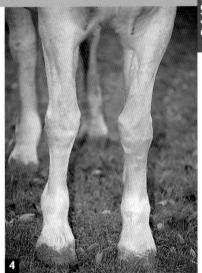

Overall impression

Stand back and look at the horse.

- Does the horse look in proportion? Do his forehand and hindquarters look balanced, as if they belong to the same horse? Or does one half look as if it belongs to another animal?
- Are his feet and limbs in proportion?
- Examine his muscle development (in particular, take a close look from behind) – is the development symmetrical?

Head & neck

These act as the horse's balancing pole so it is important that they are in proportion to the rest of his body. A large head on a long, weak neck will mean more weight is placed on the horse's forehand.

Shoulders & withers

Traditionally the ideal shoulder should have a slope of 45 degrees to the horizontal to give a good stride length, and this slope should be reflected in the hoof/pastern angle so that the concussive forces are absorbed equally throughout the limb. The withers should be well defined, allowing plenty of room for muscle attachment.

Chest

This should be broad enough to allow ample space for the heart and lungs.

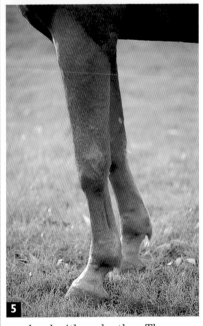

Feet

These should be a suitable size for the horse, and matching pairs. The hoof/pastern angle of the back feet should be around 50 degrees, whereas the front feet should have an angle of about 45 degrees. The height of the heel should be about half the height of the front of the foot.

Forelimbs

When viewed from the side and the front the forelimbs should be straight. Sloping backwards, forwards, or angling in or out, are all faults. The cannon bones should be short.

Hindquarters

This area is the powerhouse of the horse. Look for a rounded rump with good length from the point of hip to point of buttock. From behind check that the points of hip

are level with each other. There should also be plenty of length from the point of hip to the hock. Look at the hock from the side – it should be well defined and wide.

Once you have assessed a horse while stationary you need to see him move so that you can assess his action. Note anything which is unexpected: for example, a horse with a decent slope to the shoulder could be expected to have a good length of stride. If he doesn't you need to consider why this is the case.

To what degree is conformation considered when dealing with a problem horse?

It could be that a horse is objecting to his workload because of a problem associated with his conformation. For instance, horses are often pushed into jobs they are not suited for, and when they object they are labelled problem horses. There is no point in trying to push a horse beyond his physical or mental limits: it will only cause trouble.

Sometimes we get horses in that are supposed to be a particular breed, yet do not look as you would expect them to. If a horse is underfed and underdeveloped he cannot possibly work properly. Pain and discomfort can also mean that a horse's musculature does not develop as expected; as with every physical problem, the root cause needs to be discovered and treated.

Sometimes problems can be made worse through the horse being worked incorrectly and stressed; for example, we once saw a very talented horse that had a slight roach back, which became much more obvious as his muscles tensed up through incorrect work.

Does a horse's breeding play any part in his training?

Some breeds are more sensitive than others, and this affects how you handle them. Arabs, for instance, are not very forgiving, but once they realise you are working with them (not against them) they are very generous. Cleveland Bays have their own opinions and you have to be tactful when trying to persuade one to change his view on something. They tend to just shut down until you have worked out what you are supposed to be doing.

Mike has seen people bully even Hanoverians and Trakehners into giving in, but believes that the best way to deal with these horses is to use tact rather than brawn. They are more than capable of fighting back if someone tries to bully them.

Mike likens Irish Draughts to dolphins: 'They remind me of dolphins as they are big, soft-hearted animals and get genuinely upset when someone is being hard on them. They may fight back or may just shut down. Irish Draught horses are a lot more sensitive than their bulk would suggest.

'Thoroughbreds are much feistier, and it's easier to know what they are feeling. These horses are not as tough, either emotionally or physically, as they would like to think. You have to be more sympathetic with TBs – they are the kind of horses that would break down mentally more easily than others.'

However, the best approach with any horse is to give him the benefit of the doubt, as most horses are pretty sensitive and generous.

Q How do I assess my horse's abilities?

This can be difficult, especially if you are having problems with your horse. It might be that you are not experienced enough to bring out the best in him, or it could be that his talents fall short of your own abilities and ambitions. It is often easier for an outside person to have a clearer idea, so ask a trusted instructor or trainer for help.

Try not to get too narrow-minded about a horse's future. Sometimes people are so set on turning their horse into an eventer that they fail to notice that the horse is struggling and would be much happier doing something else. Like us, horses need to enjoy their work to get the most out of it. A horse may be bred to show jump, but it does not mean that he is going to be any good at show jumping. Just think of all the Thoroughbreds who do not make it as successful racehorses!

It is sensible for all horses, whatever their breeding, to have a good basic train-ing and from there to specialise according to their particular talents. Then, if they do not make the grade in their speciality, they at least have a good grounding and can be channelled into another area.

Be realistic about your horse and his limitations. Your cob may well love cross-country jumping, but he is unlikely to have the scope and speed needed for success in affiliated, novice level horse trials. Horses that are pushed beyond their limits do become stressed and may even sustain injuries. In some cases they break down mentally before any physical prob-lems arise.

Mike often has talented horses sent to his yard. The scenario tends to be that the horses showed promise as youngsters and were pushed to achieve. By the time they are six or seven the horses start to object and become more difficult to ride and handle. By the time they are eight they have been sold on and the new, unsuspecting owner finds she has a problem horse. These prob-lems can manifest as napping, rearing, refusing to move, refusing to jump, being vicious, and so on. The lucky horses find their way to Mike's yard where his Think Equus approach has helped many become useful riding horses.

Basically, the secret to assessing your horse's abilities lies in giving the horse the benefit of the doubt and undergoing a systematic and progressive training programme. By working the horse second by second, consolidating each step and building up the work sensibly, the horse can be allowed to develop his talents at a pace that suits him.

BE FAIR TO YOUR HORSE: LOOK AFTER HIS FUTURE

If, as a rider, you find that you have outgrown your horse, it is your responsibility to secure his future. You can do this either by keeping him and perhaps arranging for someone else to ride him, or by finding him a suitable home where he will be appreciated for what he is, not for what someone would like him to be!

Q What qualities should I look for in my instructor?

If you apply the Think Equus approach to your own training you would want:

- A sympathetic instructor who will see things from your point of view and will help you to achieve but will expect you to give 100 per cent commitment.
- Someone you trust and are happy working in partnership with.
- Someone who will work with you second by second and set you up for success.
- Someone who will reward you when you have tried, and who will badger you if you are not giving 100 per cent.
- Someone who speaks your language – this is very important, as people do differ in the way they learn. Some need to experience and feel what something is like in order to learn about the experience; others can be told about it; others need to see what it is. Most of us draw on all three sensations but have a predisposition to one of them. If your instructor knows that you are the type of person who needs to 'see' things, she can alter her language to use words that better match your requirements and therefore accelerate your learning and understanding.

Q How can I get over any riding or handling worries?

Think about how you would help your horse to cope with and beat a problem such as clipping. You would break it down into small chunks and gradually expose him to the experience, building up his tolerance until he could cope. First you would need to accustom him to the noise of the clippers close by, then the noise and feel of the clippers on him, then the clippers being used on his body, and so on.

Sometimes it helps to think of your particular riding or handling difficulty as belonging to someone else. This detachment can give you a fresh view of the problem and help you to see the solution.

If you feel that you need a really radical change of mindset then try a Neuro Linguistic Programming session. This area of psychology is being increasingly used in sports and is really useful for riders (see Appendices).

A good way to engage your horse's brain is by using different exercises such as backing between two poles

CASE STUDY

FROM NEGATIVE TO POSITIVE

Ten-year-old Newt's abundance of presence and character really attracted Hazel, even though the horse seemed to have a bit of a dodgy history! Hazel really wanted to work with Newt, despite his tenseness and the fact that he appeared to have had a lot of forced training in the past.

The problem she had not anticipated was Newt's violent negative reaction to work. In the first few days he was very worrying. He napped, reared, and tried to climb out of the school, irrespective of whether he had a rider on board or not. Hazel tried to take away a lot of pressures – but to everything she asked Newt seemed to reply, 'Make me!' He expected everything to be a fight, and his battle skills were quite impressive.

Hazel was close to giving up when she called Mike. 'The really big plus was that Mike was so positive straightaway. He made it all seem possible again,' explained Hazel. 'He helped to make the horse feel that he wanted to do the job, and instead of fighting us Newt could work out what we wanted. By taking away further pressures (including saddle and martingale!), and really believing in what he did, Mike was able to give the horse more freedom to use himself and less reason to fight.

'Positive reward for the simplest of tasks seemed to make Newt feel appreciated instead of threatened. You could really feel the horse relax just for a rub on the neck as a way of saying thank you – for example, for turning away from the gate.

'One of Newt's best features is his love of jumping. When I bought him, I was told that his problem would be rushing. Apparently it was his speed into fences that put a lot of people off buying him. Riding him over lots of small fences, initially bareback and then under saddle, and turning away on landing, rewarding and repeating, all helped Newt decide for himself that it was easier to go steadier.

'Giving him as free a rein as possible, turning rather than pulling up, gave him less to fight and he became more relaxed and confident. His love of jumping proved very useful in the early days for getting him out of a napping deadlock and getting him moving forward again.

'One of our biggest problems was major napping episodes on entering arenas at shows. So we took Newt to hired show venues, and gave the horse fun work sessions to get him more and more on our side. (Now on a good day he naps into the arena!)

'It has been, and will be, a long slow process, with still the occasional moments of mistrust. However, it's very rewarding to see an unhappy, aggressive horse loving life and work again, and being competitively successful as well.'

Newt's speed into fences had deterred a lot of potential purchasers. When a horse rushes his fences there can be many reasons why. In Newt's case both Hazel and Mike felt the horse needed to feel less pressured. However, Mike's interpretation of this went further than Hazel's: he removed the saddle and martingale!

Saddle pads and a surcingle replaced a saddle and Hazel soon found that her horse started to relax – note the lower head carriage in the second photograph

It was then a case of building up Newt's confidence in his new-found freedom so that he could move more freely but learn to steady himself as well. On landing Hazel had to make turns giving her horse as free a rein as possible. With nothing to pull against and no reason to pull, Newt learnt to do everything at a much more sensible speed

Then it was time to reintroduce the tack, keeping everything as simple as possible. Newt responded well. Initially they started over single fences

Gradually more complex questions were asked — Newt is now able to cope with combinations easily, without reverting to his old, uncontrollable behaviour. He maintains a good shape and Hazel can direct him as she wishes — and they have since achieved considerable success in both dressage and jumping competitions

3 A training blueprint

Every time you handle your horse you are teaching him something. You can teach him how to behave badly without realising it: horses can learn good and bad things equally well. How you present yourself to him is therefore vital: you want him to see you as a reliable friend who is to be trusted, who will help him. If he detects any uncertainty in you, or you let him down by acting inconsistently (perhaps by being understanding and helpful one day, and then short-tempered and overly-demanding the next) the partnership will experience problems.

Part of the Think Equus philosophy is a commitment from both parties to give 100 per cent effort. From the rider or handler's point of view this means that you must:

■ Be clear about what you are trying to achieve.
■ Communicate this effectively to your horse, at a suitable level for that particular horse at that particular time.
■ Be flexible in how you reach the objective.
■ Work second by second with your horse.

The first objective is to be clear in what you are trying to achieve. We all want a horse that is forward going, supple, obedient, well trained, responsive… a horse that is a joy to ride. How do we achieve this?

We need to understand what is meant by forward going, supple and so on. Everyone has a different interpretation, according to his or her level of experience and training. If you have only ever ridden the average riding-school horse, your idea of a forward-going horse will be totally different to the horse owner who has always had fit Thoroughbred event horses. If your experience of riding has been solely confined to hacking you may not be able to tell if a horse is supple or not. Even the question of whether a horse is responsive or not is muddied by the rider's own experiences and expectations. An experienced rider used to well-trained horses will expect merely to think about a change of direction, alter their body weight slightly, and achieve it. A novice rider would not be able to control their movements to this degree. He or she would more likely expect to give the horse a very clear signal (like a kick!) in order to get him to move. If the novice rider did this on a well-trained and sensitive horse he may well find himself on the floor!

Irrespective of whether we see ourselves as novices or experienced riders, something we can all do to improve our knowledge is to ride different horses, take lessons, watch other people ride, watch videos, watch top riders working in at shows, ask questions, discuss horses with other people… the list is endless. It is only by making an effort and gaining experience that we learn, by trying things, making mistakes, thinking about the problem and trying again. No one can expect to get things right all the time. You will also find that as you gain in experience and knowledge you will start to question some ideas that you have long held as 'truths'. This process is essential if you are to develop into a truly thinking rider and trainer.

Q Why is it important to have a horse relaxed and calm?

It is impossible for horses or humans to learn if they are anxious. When we work with our horses we are trying to progress their education, so in order for them to learn they need to be relaxed and calm. The level of relaxation is important for we do not want them to be so laid-back they are virtually asleep! This is why it is important to work with the horse second by second so that you keep him relaxed but interested. If you notice that he is becoming too laid-back you can pick up the pace of the lesson, or introduce something a little more complex so that he has to engage his brain.

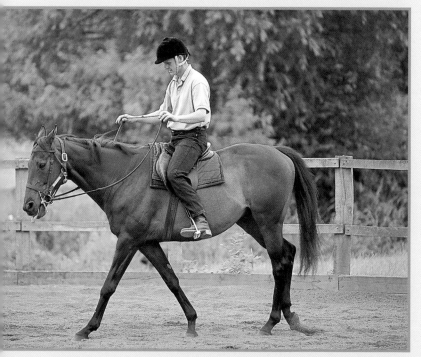

The more common problem lies in getting a horse to relax. Past experiences can create problems today: for instance, Lesley was helping an owner whose horse became incredibly uptight as soon as they entered the manège. The horse had good paces, and investigations into his past revealed that at one stage he had been pushed very hard to achieve success in the dressage arena. The horse had objected to the work and had been 'shown that the rider was boss' on several occasions. These incidents had occurred in the arena and explained the horse's current behaviour.

For a horse to relax he needs to feel secure in his environment, and the abused horse certainly did not feel happy in an arena. His mindset had to be changed, and once he was shown that his current rider and instructor were there to help and would not hit him, he made progress. For his rider this meant not grabbing hold of him and pulling back every time he started to go faster. It also meant resisting the temptation to do too much with the horse, and going back to basic training instead.

Some horses do learn very quickly, and because their brains are so active their bodies are too! To help achieve relaxation and calmness with such animals you perhaps need to introduce exercises which challenge them a little more, such as working through TTEAM labyrinths, or doing Western exercises such as backing up along an L-shaped tunnel of poles.

Both horse and rider need to be relaxed to learn and work effectively. If you tense the muscles in your legs you cannot help but walk rather stiffly. Think of your horse – if his muscles are tense he won't be able to move freely and easily!

Left: *You can see that this horse is not yet relaxed — his ears are back, his nostrils wide, and his tongue is hanging out of his mouth*

Right: *A relaxed, happy horse will be easier to train so it is important that his tack fits him well. It is crucial to select your horse's bit carefully so that he is comfortable in his mouth and able to relax his jaw. Any tightness of tension in the horse's mouth will be felt throughout the rest of his body*

Below: *This mare can get quite hyperactive. To calm her down, she is worked through exercises like this TTEAM labyrinth: halting in the labyrinth, reining back, moving forwards one step at a time, negotiating the turns slowly, and so on, all help to slow her down. She has to think about where she puts her feet. This work helps to change her mindset and get her more relaxed*

Q Can you explain 'free forward movement'?

Watch horses at liberty in a field and you will notice how different they all are. Some will have very flashy paces and appear to float above the ground; others will have a higher knee action but can still look purposeful and graceful as they move; others will have shorter strides and have to make much more effort to cover the ground. However, they are all happy to go forward freely. Sadly, once a rider is on board, a horse's movement can become much more stilted. By trying to force a horse into a shape, or by restricting it with

Mike has just started this young horse and is riding him out in a paddock for the first time. With plenty of space available Mike is able to allow the horse to find his own balance and rhythm

the hands, or by not using leg or weight aids correctly, a rider can ruin a horse's movement.

Each rider needs to be aware of how they are using their body, how they are sitting, and how they may be affecting the horse's balance and movement. This knowledge and awareness cannot be learnt from a book: you need to ride, to work on developing an independent seat and to develop your feel for what is happening beneath you as you ride.

For a horse to move forward freely he has to carry himself and his rider in the most efficient way. You can help him by sitting in the easiest place for him to carry you, usually defined as sitting over the horse's centre of gravity. As the horse moves faster so the centre of gravity shifts — the dressage rider's seat would not therefore be of any use to flat-race jockey's! Sometimes a horse needs you to sit in a

slightly different place to where you would expect. Young horses certainly find it easier to cope with a rider if the rider is positioned slightly more forward and off the back.

Apart from the physical difficulties of carrying a rider and moving forwards freely there is also the horse's instinctive behaviour to consider. Horses live in herds and move as a unit, gaining confidence and security from the presence of the other horses. It is therefore a real challenge for a young horse to learn to go forward freely on his own, and very important that trainers and riders realise this.

A problem that arises with horses of all ages is that of the rider driving into the horse's back with her seat — often because she has been taught to 'polish' the saddle with her bottom in canter! Many riders sit too heavily as they have not learnt to absorb the horse's movement through the small of their back, and encouraging them to 'polish' the saddle only makes things worse. In such circumstances it is difficult for the horse to achieve free forward movement.

The notion of going forwards must be remembered at all stages in a horse's education. Once a

Right: To encourage a horse to move forwards freely you may need to sit in a different place, that is, where the horse wants you to sit rather than where your instructor says you should sit. Often this means being slightly more forward. You can also see here that Mike is giving the rein forwards to encourage the horse to move forwards

Far right: Swinging the horse along to get him moving freely is an important part of the Think Equus way of training

young horse is going forwards problems can occur because the rider starts to think about getting the horse into an outline, and instead of riding the horse forward to the contact, starts to use the rein too much and the legs too little. Forwards, forwards, is the mantra we must all remember.

WHO IS WORKING HARDEST?

One of the easiest ways to assess whether your horse is moving forwards freely or not is to ask yourself, 'Who works hardest, my horse or me?' If the answer is 'You', then the horse is not going forwards freely. If you are working hard then it is more difficult for you to maintain a good position and to keep your balance. You should be able to tell your horse to move into a certain pace, and he should stay there without you having to constantly remind him by nagging with your legs.

Q Why are rhythm and balance important?

Rhythm is the regularity and consistency of the footfalls within a pace. If a horse can maintain a rhythm as he works in the various paces this will help his balance, which in turns helps him to use his 'engine', that is, engage his hindquarters.

To gain an understanding of rhythm a trainer would start work on the horse's trot as this is a two-beat pace and is the easiest in which to learn rhythm (for both horse and rider). The horse springs from one diagonal pair of legs to the other. Improving the trot rhythm usually helps the canter

rhythm. Canter, a three-beat rhythm, would be concentrated on next.

It is very easy to ruin a horse's walk, so work on rhythm is usually carried out in trot and canter first. Any work on the walk is best done out on hacks as the horse is probably walking out in a more relaxed and natural way. When working in the school there is the danger that the rider tries too hard and as a result restricts the horse's natural walk stride.

Horses know all about balance – they can tear around their fields, make sharp turns and stops without falling over. It is only when a rider gets on that they have to readjust to cope with this extra weight which moves around! The ridden horse

MAKE ALLOWANCES FOR YOUNGSTERS

Young horses should also be allowed to carry their heads wherever they feel comfortable. They tend to experiment with a variety of positions, sometimes carrying their heads higher than you'd like. More often, though, a young horse will carry his head and neck quite low with the nose slightly pointed forward. The head and neck are important for maintaining balance during movement, so it's best not to interfere at this stage.

learns about balance with a rider on board through a variety of exercises. The aim for the ridden, balanced horse is to maintain his way of going actively, in whatever pace and through transitions, with ease.

Young horses do eventually find a rhythm with which they are comfortable, and this occurs as the horse becomes stronger over a period of a few weeks. In the early stages of riding, a horse will change his rhythm, constantly speeding up and slowing down. A rider should allow this so that the horse can find his own rhythm and balance.

Rhythm and balance are vital foundations for a horse's work, but a rider who lacks an independent seat and control of her body can adversely affect them. Part of the Think Equus philosophy is that both parties work for the common good: the rider must constantly strive to improve her skills otherwise she will hamper the horse and reduce his ability to use himself efficiently.

Far left: This horse is not balanced: the rider is not helping him to negotiate the circle
Left: Success – Mike has got the horse moving forwards and is raising his inside hand to help the horse balance on a circle

Right: Working through trotting poles helps a horse's rhythm. Raising the poles so that they are a few inches off the ground encourages the horse to use his joints more and produces a more elevated stride

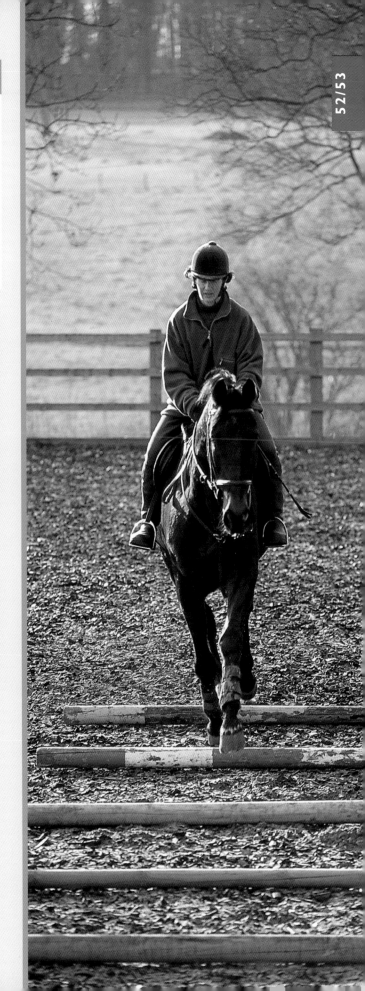

Q How can I encourage my horse to engage his hindquarters?

If you think of the horse as a car for a moment, the engine is definitely in the hindquarters. These provide the propulsive power to move the horse forwards, sideways and upwards. How far each hind leg comes under the body affects the length and power of the horse's stride. This can be affected by the horse's conformation (for example, if he has a long or a short back), and by the way in which the horse is ridden. A rider should use her legs alternately and in time with the horse's movement in order to influence the stride length. As you sit on your horse tune in to the swing of his belly – it moves from side to side, and you can feel it touching first one leg and then swinging away from the other leg. For example, as you feel the horse's belly swing away from your right leg, that is the time to apply your right leg. As the belly swings away the horse's hind leg is just coming off the ground, and if you use your leg at that precise moment you can encourage the horse to take a longer step. It's no good using your leg when you feel the horse's belly swinging into your leg as this is the point when the hind leg has been placed on the ground and you cannot influence it any more. By timing your

Above: This horse is moving forwards actively, responding well to his rider's aids and is negotiating the jumps easily. Look at how the hind leg is coming well under the horse's body to provide the propulsive power for jumping

Right: This is a good example of a horse using speed to jump – the head in the air, hollow frame and trailing hindquarters are all consequences of the horse rushing and not using herself properly

leg aids with the picking up of the horse's hind legs you can ask your horse to take longer strides.

Progressive schooling exercises will help your horse to develop the weight-carrying capacity of his hindquarters. A horse tends to carry about 60 per cent of his weight on his forehand. The purpose of schooling is to shift this weight distribution so that the horse's hindquarters become stronger and more powerful. As an example, when in collection the horse is able to lower his croup and bring his hocks more underneath him, so enabling the forehand to become lighter and the horse to carry himself and his rider much more easily.

Q How does impulsion differ from speed?

When a horse is moving actively forwards, in good rhythm and balance, and is able to react correctly and immediately to the rider's instructions, he is said to be moving 'with impulsion'. Controlled energy, which can be directed as required, would be another way of describing impulsion. It is certainly not speed, although many people – such as those who think that the only way to get over a jump is to go flat out at it! – do confuse the two terms. Working through grids is a good way of teaching a rider about impulsion: when she has her horse moving with impulsion he should find the work really easy; if the pair lack impulsion the horse will struggle to get through the grid. A horse who is moving with impulsion has a genuine desire to go forward. Think about this when you next hack out or go into an arena to school: is your horse moving with impulsion?

Q Why is suppleness so important?

In order to carry himself efficiently and perform all that is asked of him, a horse has to be supple from poll to tail (longitudinally) and from side to side (laterally). The first can be recognised as the horse moves along actively and loosely with a swinging body, and the second can be seen as the horse is equally soft whether the bend is to the right or left. A horse may soon lose suppleness if he is no longer worked or is worked incorrectly. Most horses have one side stiffer than the other. Be conscious of this and ensure that you school on both reins rather than just working on the rein which the horse finds easiest. When hacking out remember to change diagonals often if trotting and ask for a specific leg when cantering. It helps the horse if you can handle and lead him from both sides rather than just always working from the nearside.

How do you know if a horse is straight?

Dressage judges often make remarks such as 'fairly straight' and 'losing quarters to the left'. These comments show that the horse's hind legs are not following in the track his front legs are making and so he is not travelling in a straight line, whether on the straight or going around corners. Young horses in particular find it difficult to work in straight lines – it is a skill that has to be developed. Straightness is easier to achieve if the horse has good balance and is moving forward freely in good rhythm, so these schooling essentials are put into place first.

Can you explain what is meant by 'contact on the reins'?

This is the feel on the rein through the bit to the horse's mouth. The feel on both reins should be equal, and can be light without being loose providing the horse accepts the rein and is accepting rather than resistant to it. With a trained horse in self-carriage the feel on the rein can be incredibly light; one instructor Lesley knows has riders in her clinics riding with strands of knitting wool for reins. Riders and horses that are suitably prepared can ride movements in walk, trot and canter with their wool reins.

 ## Why is being 'on the bit' so difficult to achieve?

This is a term on which riders get fixated. As a result they tend to haul in the front end of the horse, trying to hold his head in by fixing their hands, and often forgetting to use their legs to keep him moving forward actively. The picture created tends to be one of tension and resistance, with both horse and rider looking uncomfortable.

Riders would be better to concentrate on getting a horse moving actively, with his hindquarters engaged, relaxed throughout his body, moving with rhythm, in balance and obediently. Once all this is in place the horse is more likely to relax his jaw and accept the bit.

It takes time to achieve straightness on the flat but the work will pay off. Just as work in-hand helps work under saddle, so flatwork helps with a horse's jumping; being able to keep your horse straight is vital

The rider's focus is also important in maintaining the line when negotiating a series of fences. It is good discipline for horse and rider to ride straight on after jumping a fence

I've backed my young horse. What should I do next to help him progress?

Free forward movement is the essential starting point in every ridden horse's career. It is vital to allow a horse to move and become comfortable carrying his rider. If you do this with a young horse you'll notice that after a few weeks his natural rhythm will be developing, as a result of his improved physical strength and an increase in his confidence and relaxation.

As rider, it's important that you help him achieve this by giving him a free rein and leaving him alone as much as possible. Riding freely requires good balance, and you should not rely on the reins or grip with the legs. You move with the horse as he moves naturally through his paces. There will be times when a young horse will lose his rhythm for a stride or two, perhaps as a result of tension if he is

LET YOUR HORSE FIND HIS OWN RHYTHM

As in so many other examples with horses, it is often better to do less than more. You have probably seen riders fiddling with a young horse to control his pace, and the youngster getting agitated and his rhythm erratic as a result. He may also start to shake his head or lean on the bit. Fiddling and so on does not help – the horse has to find his rhythm himself.

spooked by something. Alternatively, he may stumble across the ground. However, a horse will very soon recognise that it's much more efficient and easier to maintain a steady rhythm. It is his responsibility to find and maintain a rhythm that suits him best – by staying out of his way and riding him freely forward you make this easier for him.

 I do not have access to an arena. Should I start riding my young horse in an enclosed area?

Mike does not work in an arena but prefers to ride in his 3-acre paddock. He finds that schools are often too small for riding young horses. In the paddock he can make lots of changes of direction, and once he starts introducing circles into the horse's work he can ride large sweeping circles. Over time these circles can be reduced in size as the horse becomes more confident and balanced.

Mike schools all the horses that come to him in an open field, making the most of the extra space that this allows – but bear in mind the safety implications before riding a youngster in an unenclosed area

 When I ride my youngster in the school he tends to fall in around the corners.

It's often said that increased use of the inside leg can help this problem – but that's not the way to go about it.

Your horse could probably benefit from working in a larger area to develop his balance. When riding circles or corners on young horses it is not uncommon for them to fall in through the inside shoulder. When this happens most riders have a tendency to drop the inside rein and use more inside leg. Horses do find this difficult, and in Mike's experience this only makes things worse. Mike tells his riders to raise their inside hand as they make a turn. This helps a rider stay sitting correctly, which helps a young horse to balance through the bend.

There is no point in squeezing a young horse with your inside leg; you are simply giving him something to lean into. If you bump him with your leg on each stride it's easier for him to understand and respond.

 How does all this apply to older horses?

Many of the horses are sent to Mike's yard because their owners believe they have complex problems. However, the horses' difficulties often go back to something much more basic – such as the fact that they have never been taught to lead properly, or to go forwards freely. Once they have learnt to move again, or have learnt to respect their handler's personal space, or to pay attention, then the other more 'complex' problems are soon resolved.

> **GET THE BASICS RIGHT**
>
> It is really important to get the basics of any horse's education right – yet often people are so keen to press on that they ignore these, and as a result cause problems for themselves in the long term.

A horse's education is continuous: you begin on day one and continue for the rest of that horse's life. Only your own knowledge and your ability to present new things correctly limit your horse's education.

The key is to work only at the pace that each horse can cope with. There is an optimum speed that varies with each horse in each session. In addition, you have to understand the horse's physical, mental and emotional limitations. It's vital to understand how to develop each aspect of our horse in order to reach our end goal. Aim for a steady progression, a smooth learning curve.

Q What qualities do I need, as a rider and trainer?

The most important thing is to listen to your horse – he will give you constant feedback on how he feels about himself, about his work and his relationship with you. It's a case of recognising the clues and fitting them together so that you can help your horse. You'll find other tips throughout this book – such as keeping an open mind, keeping fear and doubts out of your mind, staying unemotional and detached when dealing with a horse. The power of your mind is phenomenal – and if you can use it to your advantage as a rider and a trainer you will make superb progress.

Before you start any riding session spend some time tuning in to your horse physically and mentally. Be aware of how he is using his body – does he feel as if he is taking equal strides? Does he feel stiff? Is he pushing off equally from each hind foot? Prepare yourself mentally as well by banishing other worries – you need to focus on your horse

When things do not go to plan, flexibility may be called for

A positive attitude and the ability to focus on solutions, not problems, will pay off for any rider or trainer

- A horse's natural movement can easily be hindered, especially if the horse is young and weak. Unbalanced or tight riders will interfere with a horse's movement. The key is to understand how a horse moves and then allow your body to follow the flow of the movement. Practise this on your horse – ask someone to lead him round while you sit relaxed and tune in to his movement. Once you are aware of this notice how it affects the way your body moves.
- Resist the temptation to fiddle too much – it is common to see riders taking a pull before a jump, or seesawing with the reins in a vain attempt to get their horse's head down. Excess movement from the rider just makes it more difficult for the horse to carry them efficiently.

- Be aware that you can cause your horse physical strain and injury. If you are always unbalanced, or are a tight, nervous or unsympathetic rider, your horse will have to compensate for this in the way he moves. This inevitably means he will be using himself less efficiently and is more likely to strain his muscles.

- Your horse may also be affected psychologically if he experiences physical discomfort every time he is ridden. This could result in him having a negative attitude to work, which inevitably means that people get tougher on him; as a result he has to harden up to deal with this, and a downward spiral begins.

- Do not try to hold a young horse together – he will be far too big and strong for you to do this, and he needs to learn to carry himself anyway. Initially a young horse will be weak and unsteady with a rider, but it is his responsibility to carry himself.

- All any rider can do is stay balanced and keep out of the horse's way as much as possible. This applies when riding young and old horses. It is your job to stay balanced and to maintain your position without relying on the reins for support or gripping with your legs. It is your job to direct and enthuse the horse, but it is the horse's job to carry the rider.

- You may make the horse's job easier by leaning forward slightly and taking the weight off the back, for example when riding a young horse or a horse that is stiff or weak in its back.

- Do not have the rein contact too tight with a young horse, or irritate him with constant kicks to his side. If he feels restricted he may tense up and lose his natural forward movement. If really upset a youngster could buck or rear.

- Most young horses move forward quite freely when first ridden, but lots of people try to slow this movement down by pulling on the reins. Don't do this, but let the horse move at whatever pace he needs to (set yourself and your horse up for success and be safe by working in an arena or small paddock). If the horse goes too fast and worries you then direct

him through a few changes of direction. To make the turns easier for himself the horse has to slow down – so in effect he is deciding to slow down rather than you pulling on him.

- Do not pull on a young horse's mouth. Use the changes of direction as described above. Never pull on both reins at once as this will feel restrictive to him and he's likely to increase speed to get away from the restriction.

- Make a young horse's lessons fun – give him plenty of changes of direction, work in different places. Make life stimulating, not boring, or it will be all too easy for a youngster to switch off from work.

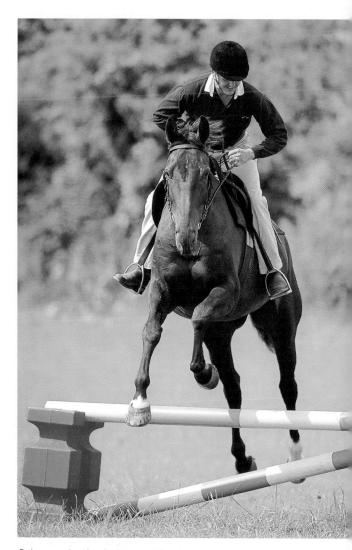

Riders need to be thinking people, who can turn a situation around and set the horse up for success

LOOSENING THE MUSCLES OF THE BACK

Mike was called out to see this horse as the rider was having trouble hacking out. The horse was becoming increasingly nappy and was starting to rear. In Mike's experience there is always a reason for this – it's just a case of finding it. He suggested that they view the horse working in the school, as the horse was supposedly happy to work in the arena. Within a couple of minutes Mike could see that the horse was not enjoying life but was just dealing with it as best he could.

Mike watched the owner riding this horse in the school, and it was clear that although the horse was obedient he lacked sparkle and was operating in an almost mechanical way. The horse was talented and had been schooled with the help of a dressage trainer but did not look as if he was enjoying life. He had always had a roach back, and the owner had commented that this had gradually become worse. The muscles in the horse's back were actually rock hard

◄ **Mike's Solution**

Mike got on and, instead of riding the horse in the way in which the animal expected, gave him his freedom. The horse was very unsure about this at first.

▶ Within a short while the horse started to enjoy this new way of riding – his stride length improved and he started to push off from behind more.

◄ Mike ensured that he kept out of the horse's way at every pace – this was a real change for a horse that had been used to being drilled and ridden in quite a dogmatic way.

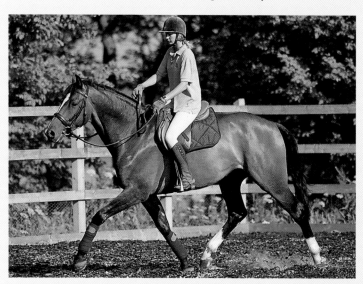

▲ Back on board, the owner can feel the difference in the horse's way of going. The stride is greatly improved; the horse is much freer all over his body; he is relaxed in his mouth and the muscles around his roach back are much softer as the tension is disappearing.

In order to get this horse back on track he needs much more of this looser, freer way of riding to release his body and his mind. Like many talented horses he is finding it hard to deal with the demands being placed upon him, and his nappy behaviour was just his way of communicating that all was not well in his world.

CASE STUDY

HELPING SAMMY OVERCOME DEPRESSION

If it is possible for a horse to suffer bouts of depression, that was the problem that blighted the life of Sammy, a handsome 16hh Irish Draught x Thoroughbred.

When Sammy was bought by riding-school owner Anna Smart as a 10-year-old, she found him very introverted. He took little interest in his surroundings and grazed alone in the field, away from the other horses. However, he was friendly and affectionate, and Anna felt sure that he would make a kind, willing school horse once he'd had time to settle in.

Sammy displays extreme behavioural problems

When Anna first rode Sammy out on his own, he refused to pass the yard gate, planted his feet and violently shook his head. When she pushed him on he threatened to rear. The ride had to be abandoned, but this behaviour was repeated each time Anna attempted to ride. Sammy would stick his chin into his chest with his head virtually on the floor and then jerk it around. He didn't head shake at any time other than when he was ridden – it was almost as though it was a nervous twitch.

Anna decided to take Sammy right back to basics, with lungeing and loose-schooling work in the manège. He didn't head shake much on the lunge, but as soon as Anna took to the saddle, the head shaking started again. Anna sensed that Sammy's behaviour wasn't malicious, but rather due to him being grossly unhappy about being ridden. She had his teeth and back checked to rule out the possibility of pain, but still couldn't get to the root of the problem.

By this time the children's summer holidays had begun and, as the riding school was going to be busy for a few weeks, Anna turned Sammy out to rest. She later resumed the lunge work and, when his behaviour took yet another dive, decided to seek Mike's help.

Mike's Solution

Mike recommended that Sammy should spend a couple of weeks at his yard and Anna decided that Sammy was worth it.

'When I first began to work with Sammy he seemed very calm,' says Mike, 'I could see in his eye that something was going on in his head, yet the rest of his body appeared expressionless. I got the feeling he wasn't afraid, like so many of the other behaviour cases I come across. Nor was he calculating ways to manipulate me, like some of the older, more hardened horses I see might do.

'He seemed perfectly willing to do everything I asked him to do from the ground. I could back him up, stop him, move his quarters over and so on. I decided the only way to see what all the fuss was about was to get up on his back and see what he came up with. Within a few seconds I could feel his personality begin to change. I asked him to move forward with a little bit of leg, and instantly he objected violently by pinning his ears back and plunging his head all the way to the ground.

'I knew that this instant was a crucial point in our relationship. If I did what most riders would have done in Sammy's past – grabbed hold of his head and given him a big kick – he would simply view me as another rider adding to his problems. I didn't quite know why he was objecting so violently, but I knew the key with Sammy was going to be to ask less rather than more.

'Instantly Sammy began to think of me differently. A paradigm shift had occurred and you could see the cogs turning in his head. It was as if he was thinking, "Maybe all riders aren't the same and I don't need to get the first word in". It was incredible – within 10 minutes he was moving forward willingly from the leg and turning left and right pretty much without objection.

'He still insisted on having his head right down on the ground and was still shaking it quite violently. At this stage I just let him get on with it, giving him the freedom to take as much of the rein as he needed but very gently coaxing each change of direction from him.

'After 10 minutes of riding Sammy with his chin bouncing off the ground I decided to give him the benefit of the doubt. I took the saddle and bridle off and rode him from the headcollar. After all, he could be experiencing pain in his mouth from the bit or in his back from the saddle. Unfortunately this made no difference at all. He obviously had his own reasons for going like this and I just had to respect that.

'I was convinced that within a few days he'd realise the best way of carrying himself and bring his head up to a normal position. My priority for the moment was to keep his perception of me positive, and this meant giving him as much freedom as reasonably possible.

'Within three or four days I was riding him in walk, trot and canter around the paddock, still on the buckle end of the rein, and eventually his head began to come up to a more normal position. I had given him complete freedom to experiment with his own head position and finally he settled on looking like a normal horse, which I suppose is what you'd expect. He discovered this for himself, and so it was much more acceptable to him. Even the head shaking stopped and Sammy's personality was altogether more positive and much more expressive.'

Ten days later

'I was amazed when I went to visit Sammy at Mike's yard after 10 days,' says Anna. 'His head was up, his ears were pricked and he was interested in his surroundings again. When Mike rode him he was lively and forward going and the head shaking had stopped – it was wonderful to see him looking so happy and relaxed. I hadn't realised how unhappy he'd been and had just assumed this was his personality.

'The biggest surprise came when we got Sammy home. Before, he would ignore the other horses and go off and graze on his own, but this time we let him go and he tore off round the field. He started playing with the other horses and got straight in there with the rest of the herd. He had never shown any interest in them before so it was fantastic to see him galloping about and playing. I had no idea he could shift that fast!'

'When Sammy first arrived at my yard I think his attitude to life was very negative,' says Mike. 'He

Low head carriage like this is a normal relaxed response from a horse given a long rein, but Sammy's reaction to being ridden was a sign of his severe depression

didn't know why he was depressed – he just was. I'm pretty sure his head shaking (as is probably the case with all other head shakers) was due to nerves and stress.'

Now, Sammy has a totally different attitude to life. He is confident around people and horses and hacks out happily. For Anna, the challenge is to carry on with Mike's work.

Mike says, ' I work from whatever level a horse is at and get them to a point where the owner can continue. This is where Sammy is now. My work is not about offering a "quick fix", but is about getting a horse from negative behaviour back to zero, and from there into positive behaviour.'

4 Problems on the flat

It is worth remembering that riding is a privilege, not a right, and we should never forget this when dealing with horses. The Think Equus approach is that both horse and rider have a responsibility to each other, and from the rider's point of view this means keeping out of the horse's way so that he can do his job (carry the rider) as easily as possible. It is our job to be balanced and to allow the horse to move. When riders are too dominant various problems can arise: a horse may become nappy, or refuse to go forward. Mike has a technique to get such a horse moving again, which involves swinging your arms and legs in an exaggerated fashion. While this is a useful exercise for encouraging young or nappy horses to move forward freely, it's not ideal during your first dressage test. However, the sequence Mike has advised is:

- Hands swing left as the near fore comes off the ground.
- Right leg used as the off hind leaves the ground.
- Hands swing right as the off fore comes off the ground.
- Left leg used as the near hind leaves the ground (this should be applied at all times, albeit in a less exaggerated way).

As you both gain experience and confidence you will swing along easily with your horse, and as time goes on your job is merely to allow him his freedom of movement. As a result you'll appear to be sitting still, when actually you're allowing your body to maintain its position as your horse's body moves.

Experienced riders never sit still on a horse – it only looks like that. The aids from an expert rider on an educated horse may look invisible, but the body, legs and hands are moving all the time. If you do sit still on a horse he will find it tricky to carry you and won't be able to move naturally.

Another important point to remember is not to make the mistake of kicking with both legs simultaneously. If you consider the arm-and-leg swinging sequence, the double-sided kick may help one side of the horse to move, but it shuts down the other side at the same time. The effect is cancelled out and there is no free, forward movement.

Q How do I control the situations that my horse and I face?

In a word, politely. Whenever you control a situation – be it deciding a route on a hack, or choosing a way round a cross-country course – set up each situation to give the horse the best chance to succeed.

If, for example, you have a young horse who has never jumped before, start with tiny fences that he can cope with easily. If a horse is scared of traffic, choose a route along quiet country lanes with wide verges. That way you will avoid a drama and enjoy a successful outcome instead, which you can then thank the horse for.

Under the Think Equus philosophy both parties are expected to contribute equal shares to the partnership in order that the relationship grows

SWINGING A HORSE ALONG

Riding loose is an art, which often has to be learnt. Many people think they are riding loosely, but to the horse it feels tight and restrictive. During a lesson we often get riders to swing their hands and legs, co-ordinating them with the natural swing of a horse's body movement. You can do the same with your hands to follow the natural swing of the horse's head and neck (left to right like the pendulum of a clock). As you use your right leg, swing your left hand away from the neck (be careful that you do not pull backwards – just open the hand and arm out so that the rein is taken away from the neck).

This is so simple, yet it can vastly improve a horse's stride length. Once you and your horse have got the hang of this you can refine the movement so that it is much subtler. You will still be using alternate leg and rein aids, but almost invisibly. Good riders appear to be sitting still, but actually there is a lot of movement going on in order to absorb the movement of the horse. If you cast your mind back to learning to ride you can probably recall how by trying hard to sit still to the trot you become tense and bounced around even more.

You can use this swinging the horse along technique to achieve transitions: for example, build up the walk until over a few strides the horse moves naturally into trot, and the same from trot to canter. This is the best way for a young horse to learn about transitions as it keeps everything smooth and natural. You have to stay balanced and follow the horse's movement.

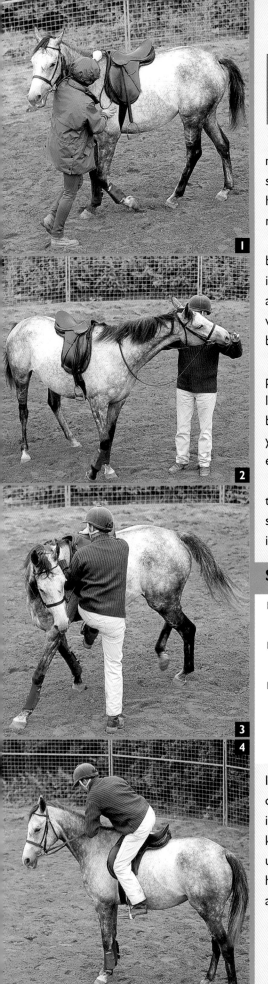

My horse has become increasingly difficult to mount.

You say that she has had very little work for a couple of years; she may feel that life was fine as it was, thank you very much! However, something else could be causing the problem. Perhaps her saddle is hurting (horses change shape and saddles must be checked regularly); maybe she is not enjoying her work; maybe she is simply misbehaving.

As she has been off for such a long time she will need to be brought back into work slowly and carefully, initially with lots of walking, building up the length of time she is ridden. This will help to harden her legs, and long, slow exercise uses up fat. If you are trying to do too much with her, too soon, she can only let you know by misbehaving – such as being fidgety when you are trying to mount.

Whatever the reason for her behaviour, the way to overcome the problem is the same. However, if poor saddle fit or an unfair workload is at the root of the problem you must deal with these issues before employing the following technique to mount. Make sure that you set up a suitable environment before you start work – make it easy for her to succeed.

At the moment she is causing you to move around as you attempt to get on her. You need to change the balance so that you stand still while she moves around. She will soon learn that being difficult to mount involves her expending a lot of energy for little benefit and will stand still.

SETTING UP A SUITABLE ENVIRONMENT

- Make everything as safe as you can – so work in a school or an enclosed area to start with.
- Do not work on a hard or concrete surface, as the risk of injury is increased if either you or your horse slips and falls.
- Avoid having other people holding on to your horse as she may well feel she is being outnumbered and pressured. In any case, you cannot rely on having other people around every time you want to get on your horse.

If you are a working horse owner you will be familiar with the scenario of having to grab a ride before work. Imagine the frustration you'd feel if your already hectic schedule was further pressured because you knew you'd have a problem getting on your horse! It's a common situation. The mare shown here was brought to one of Mike's clinics, as her owner just could not get on without lots of help. If no help was available she could not ride!

5

6

This page:

5 Then it was time for her owner to try, adopting Mike's technique of insisting that if the horse moves, she moves around the rider

6 The mare realises that her owner has now wised up as well, and stops to allow the rider to mount

7 Now there is a bigger test – can the owner maintain her cool and use the same techniques in the wide expanse of the paddock?

8 Success – now, whenever she needs to, this rider can get on her horse, without help

7

Opposite:

1 This is typical – the mare moves around all over the place while the owner struggles, unsuccessfully, to get on. Although she had sought advice from her instructor nothing had worked. The only way this rider could mount was if a couple of people could be found to hold her horse while she got on. Not a very practical solution!

2 Mike explained that while the owner was doing all the moving the horse was benefiting greatly from the situation. The mare did not have to expend much energy at all yet she could easily avoid being taken out for a ride. Mike

changed the rules – he refused to move and let the mare move instead

3 Even when he had his foot in the stirrup ready to mount, Mike ensured that he hardly moved. The mare tried to move, but by keeping the nearside rein shorter and bending the mare round to the left Mike ensured that she had to walk around him in a circle

4 It did not take long for the mare to realise that she was working hard and she still had not got rid of Mike. There he was, alongside her, and not at all fazed by her activities. As she was deriving no benefit from moving around the mare stood while Mike mounted

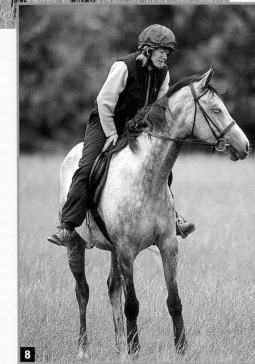

8

Q My new horse has started to buck. What can I do?

Firstly, it is important to check that the problem is not pain related. Even if the horse has suffered back pain in the past, which has now been resolved, he may still fear the thought of pain – or he may have simply discovered that bucking is a good trick for cutting short a schooling session or hack.

Once you have been able to rule out pain as a cause, you need to deal with the problem itself. If Mike knows that a horse is prone to violent bucking fits, he will employ a special pre-mounting technique.

PRE-MOUNTING TECHNIQUE

- Rather than mount up straight away, Mike stands at the horse's shoulder and bounces around at his side without actually getting on, just as he does when preparing young horses to be backed.
- Once the horse is relaxed he will belly over at the horse's withers.
- When the horse is ready, Mike will put his left foot in the stirrup and then swing his right leg over. This technique often throws the horse. After all, life for him is usually pretty simple: he bucks, his rider gets off. Here Mike is doing something that feels different. It knocks the horse off guard and gets him thinking about Mike instead of trying to get rid of him.
- Mike won't put his leg over the horse's back until he can sense that it is safe to do so. He sticks with the pre-mounting work and gauges the horse's reactions.

Whenever Mike works with horses he is always searching for a level that is one below the point at which the horse will freak out. This way, he can teach the horse and gain his trust without the situation turning into a traumatic experience.

That's why this pre-mounting work is so effective with a bucker. Instead of jumping straight on and riding out the bucks, Mike approaches the situation more intelligently, working with rather than against the horse. The horse will soon realise that by bucking he is expending more energy than Mike, and it's pointless as Mike is posing no threat, and is not asking him to work hard.

Right from the start Mike makes it clear to the horse that it's easier for him to co-operate than buck. Mike gives him an

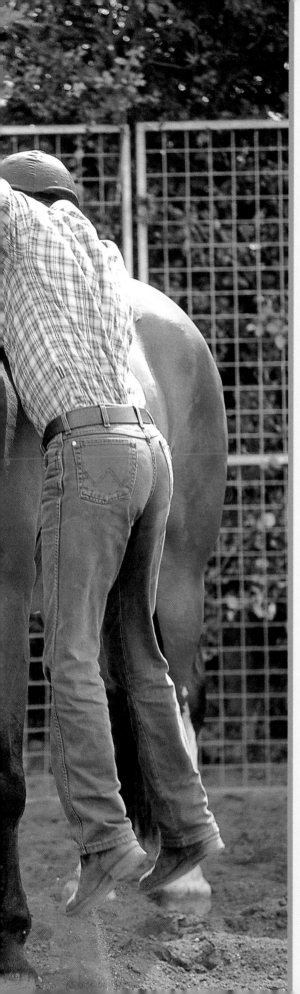

incentive to work with him – less work – and this will always appeal to a horse's nature. Horses are simple creatures; they like an easy life. Show them a way to achieve this and they will be grateful.

If you spend time on this pre-mounting exercise the horse will soon figure that trying to move away and waste energy on a bucking fit is not such a good idea. He will realise that it is a better to stand, relax and be polite. Once you have reached this stage you can mount up.

If a horse has a tendency to buck violently once you are in the saddle, you need to diffuse the situation. Every horse will set himself up by taking one quick stride before he actually bucks, so don't give him the opportunity. The second you feel him getting ready to explode smoothly draw him onto a circle, or part of a circle, and keep changing direction. This circle work will enable you to gain the horse's attention and persuade him to stop and listen to what you want, as opposed to focusing his attention on trying to get rid of you.

Remember too that when you are riding a horse with a potential to buck you need to work on keeping him relaxed. A scared, panicked horse will run and buck. However, if you can keep a horse's mind occupied, he will be more inclined to stop and think about what he's doing. So keep your leg and rein aids light, make lots of changes of direction, and keep the pace of the lesson active to give the horse plenty to think about.

REMEMBER BODY LANGUAGE

You can tell a lot about your horse's frame of mind from his facial expressions and the way he moves. So, if you are working with a horse that bucks, learn to read his actions and act accordingly. Never push a situation so far that the horse reacts violently, but find a middle ground within which the horse will tolerate adjustments to the balance of the relationship. Watch for signs that the horse is getting agitated – wild eyes, tense body language – and also signs that he is starting to relax – the eyes go soft, his head will drop, and he will start to lick and chew.

When Mike is starting a young horse he goes through the pre-mounting technique to relax the horse and prepare him for the new sensation of the rider's weight across, and then on, his back. It is also a good technique for horses with a tendency to buck

Q How do I stop a horse rearing while I'm riding?

Obviously, pain or discomfort can be a reason for rearing, as with bucking, so it is wise to ask a vet to check your horse over. If he gets the all clear, you need to get to the root of the problem itself. A horse often learns to rear once he has exhausted all other possibilities. Consider this scenario:

- You take your horse for a hack, and you come across a scary-looking 'men at work' sign, complete with a couple of cones.
- He is genuinely nervous of passing this, so he comes to a halt while he considers the options. It's worth remembering that a horse's natural instinct is to run away from any scary object rather than rationalise and deal with it. So all of his reflexes are saying 'Run'.
- You, meanwhile, know it is a harmless road sign and give your horse a hefty kick to send him on.
- He then chooses one of several options. He literally closes his eyes and leaps past, hooks off to the left or right in a bid to escape, or runs backwards.
- This inevitably leads to a battle. You may well manage to hang on to your horse and bully him past the scary object, but he hasn't learned to deal with it.

Think of it in human terms. You may be scared of spiders: someone marches up to you with a big, hairy tarantula in their hand, and you, in turn, shriek and run off. But if that person approached the situation more sympathetically, stood a distance away from you with the spider and asked you to take a look and rationalise your fears, you would be calmer. You might not want them to walk right up to you, but you would be OK with them closing the distance up to a couple of feet.

You could then work on rationalising your fear. Eventually you might pluck up the courage to stand next to the spider. By this stage you will have learned to cope with your fear as opposed to running off and not dealing with it.

If we reconsider the horse and the road sign, this horse has not been given the chance to rationalise his fears. So, when you approach the road sign again on the following day, he thinks, 'Uh-oh, not only is this horse-eating beast still here but it's bad news from her up there too'. As a result he stops at a distance a couple of strides further away from the sign than yesterday, and a repeat performance of kicking and spooking ensues.

In extreme cases such a situation can spiral out of control to the point where the horse sees you approach with the saddle, associates you riding him with the scary horse-eating monster, and refuses to even leave the stable. His behaviour is labelled as dangerous when really he is just confused and frightened.

This may be an extreme example, but it leads back to the rearing question. Once the horse has exhausted the possibilities of going back, sideways or standing stock still in such a situation, he remembers there's one other way he hasn't tried yet – going up in the air. Rearing is often a developed habit which the horse attempts as a last resort, but, like all learned behaviour, if the horse gets the result he wants – he goes home – then it has worked.

REARING WORKS FOR SOME HORSES...

Rearing is essentially an excellent way of ditching the rider and cutting short the ride. If a horse learns the art of going up in the air he will try it whenever he faces a situation which he feels he can't handle.

Mike has dealt with rearers who have discovered that it's a good – and quick – way of getting rid of people. One horse he worked with went straight up in the air the second Mike got on. The rear was not provoked: the horse merely wanted rid of him. Instead Mike stayed on – which took the horse by surprise – and 20 minutes later the horse was calm, relaxed and happy. His rearing wasn't fear related but a learned reaction in order to get his own way.

With horses that rear because they are worried and anxious, the trick is to take the horse to that crucial point, one below the point at which he will freak out and rear. This helps the horse face up to his fears and deal with them without the situation turning into a drama. However, it takes an expert to gauge this.

When dealing with a nervous rearer, Mike is sympathetic, but not so sympathetic that he can't get the job done. At the same time he is communicating to the horse that this behaviour is not acceptable. There is no place in the world for a horse that rears and he has to learn that. Mike gives the horse every chance to get over his problem and keeps the training session as interesting as possible to keep the horse's mind occupied. The rest is up to the horse. At the end of the day, he is a horse and horses have to be ridden.

Mike sees it as his job to show the horse that life is easier if he doesn't rear, and the horse's job to accept this and deal with it.

A horse can learn to cope with 'scary' objects if given the chance

Q I'm told that my horse 'drops behind the bridle'. Can you explain this term?

The phrase 'dropping behind the bit' or bridle is when a horse evades the bit by tucking his nose in closer to his chest. Evasion only occurs when a horse becomes unhappy with the way he is being asked to work and finds a way out of it. In this case he relieves the pressure of the bit by bringing his mouth closer to the rider, causing the reins to go slack and evading the action of the bit. It often happens when a horse feels uncomfortable in his mouth, usually because of a rider's strong hands.

A rider experiencing this must release his hands and get a horse reaching and moving forward on a loose rein. This will cause the horse's head to come up, and from here you can begin to bring the horse's head into the correct position so that his face is slightly in front of the vertical. This must only be done with a light even contact. Different riders each have their own concept of what contact should be. We believe the feel with a horse's mouth should be no more than the feel you would use to hold a small child's hand. There are many evasions a horse can use

MYLER BIT CLINICS

Choosing the right bit for your horse is vitally important. Dale Myler, one of the Myler bit company's founders, worked with several horses at a demonstration we attended recently, watching how they reacted to their normal bit. He then used Myler bits instead, and in each case effected a considerable improvement in the horse's acceptance of the bit, level of relaxation and way of going. He told the audience that Myler bits were not magic items to bring about changes in the horse's training but that they did enable the horse to be comfortable and relaxed so that the rider could then train the horse. Sometimes the only difference between one bit and another was in allowing slightly more room for the tongue, yet the effect upon the horse's way of going was dramatic.

to get away from the contact of the bit and the key is to ride in a way that keeps horses happy so they don't want to evade a rider.

As always, when a horse is fussy in his mouth or is not accepting the bit properly, it is worth having the teeth and mouth checked. Every horse's mouth is different, so it is important that the type and size of the bit is suitable for the individual. Some horses have thick tongues and may have difficulty if the bit does not allow the tongue to lie comfortably. The bars in the mouths of horses that are well bred tend to be narrow and only thinly covered with skin – these bars will be even more sensitive and the horse will immediately feel pain from a bit that pinches, or is badly made and has rough edges or surfaces.

The conformation of the horse's mouth also needs to be considered; if the horse has a mouth with a low roof he could be in considerable discomfort if a bit with a port was used. Selection of the correct bit is essential, and minor details can make a huge difference to the horse.

Q When and why should draw reins be used?

Draw reins should never be used. They use force to draw the horse's head into an unnatural position, often causing a horse to go over-bent and to lose his natural movement. When a horse has been schooled in draw reins he is often heavy on the forehand and is what is best described as 'jammed' into an outline. Such horses also have small underdeveloped quarters with an overdeveloped front. They look like their front doesn't match the back.

It's important to allow a horse to find his own way of carrying a rider and all horses, if ridden correctly, will eventually lower their heads and round their backs to carry a rider naturally and efficiently.

If a rider can't get a horse to come into an outline naturally while being ridden, then he should take the horse's schooling back a stage (to long-reining) to get him working from behind and developing his top line without a rider.

Q My horse swishes his tail when I do any schooling. Why, and does it matter?

Tail swishing can be interpreted as a sign of resistance or anger. It may be that your horse does not want to do whatever you are asking, perhaps because he is bored or cross, or maybe because he associates the movement with some discomfort. Look at the picture of your horse as a whole to work out what is happening.

The Think Equus way of thinking is to give the horse the benefit of the doubt, so you would first eliminate any potential problem areas:

- Check the fit of his tack, the rider's seat and application of the aids, possible muscle problems, and so on.
- Do you school too often and for too long?
- Is your schooling challenging and progressive or repetitive and boring?
- Could you add variety by schooling out on hacks or working in a paddock rather than an arena?
- Can you learn from other disciplines, such as Western riding or TTEAM, and add in polework to challenge your horse's brain as well as body?
- Perhaps you should work your horse in-hand for a change?

With a little imagination schooling can be fun for horse and rider. Organise your horse's workload so that he has fun and learns and has variety in his work. If he is free from pain and enjoying himself then signs of evasion and resistance such as tail swishing should decrease.

A horse's resistance under saddle may be caused by an injury or poorly fitting tack, but a change in routine may be the solution for a horse that's bored of schooling

Should young horses be ridden in a different way to older ones?

Yes, definitely. Riding a young horse requires very subtle movements. You can't use conventional leg aids on a young horse; they will mean nothing to him. Instead you must find a way of achieving a movement, and then associate an aid with it so you can cue the same movement again in future.

STAY IN BALANCE WITH YOUR HORSE

Riding freely requires good balance. You must move with the horse and make it his responsibility to find and maintain the rhythm that suits him best. Avoid gripping with your legs or hanging onto the reins, but instead stay in balance with him so he can find his own way.

The trick is in knowing exactly when to deliver the aid so that the horse learns to associate it with the right movement. For example, the aid for trot must be given the second the horse moves up a pace. If you give the aid while the horse is walking and nothing happens, he will associate it with walk.

Another important point to remember is never to squeeze your legs on the horse simultaneously as this feels like tension and may cause him to panic. Gently start a youngster with your lower leg while loosely directing him with your rein.

Once you have got the hang of this you can allow your legs and arms to swing in time as explained earlier. This will make it easier for the horse to carry you.

When working with young horses Mike always adopts the Think Equus approach of never pushing a horse to the point where he will freak out, but rather working at a level below that. Instead of plonking himself on a young horse and letting him career round the school bucking, Mike takes things one tiny step at a time so that the horse learns to accept a rider peacefully. There is no need for fireworks. If you have built up your horse's acceptance of the rider slowly and gently he should not feel the need to explode.

Once you have reached the point where your horse is happy to have you on board, the next stage is to help him achieve a free, forward movement. You can do this by giving him a loose rein and leaving him alone wherever possible so he can develop his own natural rhythm.

This pony has become quite a handful for his young owner when they are in open spaces. He's a forward-going pony who likes to get on with things his way. However, when his rider asks him to behave differently he can be quite opinionated! At one of his clinics Mike showed the young rider how to avoid getting into a pulling contest with her pony and to direct his energy and enthusiasm into forward movement that she could control

Q What can I do about napping?

Most people interpret napping as bad behaviour, but Mike sees it as a result of a communication breakdown. By spooking at an object out on a hack a horse is trying to tell you that he is sceptical about it. What he needs is sympathetic handling, but what he often gets instead is a dig in the ribs. This lack of empathy and understanding often leads to more serious problems, so it is worth taking time out to study why horses nap and how you can help them deal the situation.

If a horse is spooky and nervous by nature you can help to build his self-confidence by setting challenging hazards – such as a pile of plastic or some barrels – in a safe environment, such as a school or enclosed field. By creating a safe working environment the horse has a chance to deal with whatever is frightening him without the situation spiralling out of control.

PRACTISE IN SAFETY AT HOME

■ Lead or ride the horse around the school and allow him plenty of time to look at and touch the scary object. He will most probably come to a halt a few feet away from it, plant his feet and give it a good look. This is perfectly natural.

■ Let him take his time, have a sniff if he wants, and then turn him away. This will help to build his confidence. He has had a look but you haven't asked him to get uncomfortably close, and he will be reassured by this.

■ After a few minutes go back and let him have another look. Keep your reins loose, and don't squeeze with your legs. Keep all your aids light, sit light and balanced in the saddle and be sympathetic to your horse's feelings. You know that it's only a bit of old plastic, but to him it's a potential killer lying in wait. Consider his fears and work with him to overcome them.

■ Eventually, your horse will creep closer and closer to the scary obstacle and, by learning to accept this terrifying thing, will gain confidence in himself.

If you are leading the horse past or through something scary, position yourself out in front of the horse and make it clear where you want him to go. Each time he makes a step in the right direction praise him. If he doesn't try, get after him. Make it clear that you are there to help him crack his fears – but that the process requires some effort from him too.

By setting out the rules clearly you make it easy

When a horse is nappy and refuses to go where directed this is usually caused by a breakdown in communication between horse and rider

for the horse to make the right decision. If a horse is genuinely worried you obviously need to be sympathetic, but not so sympathetic that you don't get the job done.

Work like this in an arena will really help to crack a horse's nervousness, and it is ideal for all young or nervous types. While you can never totally change a horse's character, you can increase his confidence levels and give him a bolder outlook on life. So the next time a carrier bag makes your horse jump he will spook at it, then rationalise the situation and deal with it himself.

Q How can I get my horse to go through puddles? I ride her straight at them but she always dodges out to the side.

The fact that your horse will not get her feet wet may not sound like a big deal but it is something that you should address. If she cannot cope with this issue you will probably find at some point that she will not deal with ditches, or going into water jumps, and so on.

You have to help your horse face up to her problem and show her that it is OK. You could work on this problem at home by putting a piece of plastic on the ground and asking her to walk over this. You could do this exercise in-hand first and then under saddle. Her initial reaction is bound to be one of suspicion – let her take her time to investigate the monster. You might find that she tries to block the problem out altogether and just turns away from it. If this happens, keep turning her back and presenting her to the plastic again. Don't get angry: just correct her and show her that she has to deal with the problem. If she does try, by lowering her head to sniff at it, or pawing at it, or taking a step towards it, then praise her by rubbing her on the head or neck. Make her feel good about her achievement. It might only seem a small step to you but it's a much bigger issue to her. Eventually she will step over, probably in a great rush, or may even jump it. Tell her she's good and then present her again. You want her to step over the plastic slowly – doing everything in a rush is rather like you putting your hands over your eyes to avoid seeing something that upsets you. By rushing the horse is not really accepting and facing up to the problem.

1 *Exercises such as asking a horse to walk over plastic on the ground encourage the horse to think and rationalise her fears rather than just running off. Here you can see the horse thinking about the problem – as a result Mike gives her the time without interfering at all*

2 *Now she's really making an effort – you want the horse to walk calmly over the plastic rather than rush*

3 *As an extra element has been added – the poles – the mare is more suspicious and this time jumps the plastic, giving it plenty of air. She is asked this question again until she can calmly pop over it*

4 *For balance, the mare has to learn to deal with the problem by approaching from either rein. Although she is accepting from one direction she has a different viewpoint from this way. Now the process begins again, cueing one foot to move at a time, getting her to try to deal with her problem*

Q How do I deal with my young horse when he plants himself and refuses to move?

The answer here is to cue a movement – any movement, be it sideways or forwards – and then praise the horse for it. Rather than kick with both legs simultaneously, which will merely shut off one side of the horse, you need to get one foot to move. Do this by opening the inside rein and using the opposite leg to bump start some movement. Once you have some movement going you can swing your horse along, as described in the panel on p69.

Above: *This is an older horse – she has learnt that planting herself and refusing to move has paid dividends as she has not had to deal with her problem In her case, once some movement has been achieved she has to be ridden forwards strongly. With a young, anxious horse more sympathetic riding would be called for*

Q What should I do if my horse starts to go backwards as an evasion?

Mike uses a device called a 'whip-wop' in situations where a horse has learned to run backwards to avoid something that is worrying him. Using one hand, Mike simply swishes this short piece of rope from side to side as soon as the horse takes a step back. Thanks to its peripheral vision the horse can see the rope and will move away from this. As soon as you feel your horse take a step forward then stop using the rope.

Q How can I stop my horse rushing when schooling?

When a horse goes too fast most riders react by taking a pull on the reins. As a result, a battle starts to develop – the horse rushes more, the rider tries harder by pulling harder, and so it goes on. Instead of pulling back on the reins keep your rein contact light and use changes of direction and circles to slow your horse. If necessary ride him towards the arena side and then at the last minute ask him to go left or right – as the horse turns he has to slow himself down. As he slows down you can take advantage of this fact and ask for another change of direction or a circle – anything rather than go in a straight line which will simply allow your horse to get faster and faster. The biggest obstacle is for the rider to overcome her mindset and to keep the contact light. If your horse has nothing to pull against he will stop pulling.

This young rider has a problem with her Arab pony – she finds it difficult to control the pony out in the open, as the pony becomes stronger and stronger.

1 The rider is experiencing problems after only a few minutes in the paddock. Her pony is getting stronger and more onward bound, and the rider's natural reaction is to take a pull on one rein

2 Here we can see that the rider is being pulled forward by the pony. The rider has a strong hold on her pony but naturally the pony pulls back and is able to wrench the rider forward. In any battle of strength a pony or horse will always win so there is no point going down this route

3 Mike gets on and explains how to use lots of turns and circles to regulate the pony's pace. As soon as he feels the pony start to get faster Mike uses a turn or circle to cause the pony to slow down

4

4 *The owner tries this, with Mike reading the situation before she does and helping her to time the turns and changes of direction. The rider really has to focus on what her pony is doing and learn to feel the second the pony starts to increase his pace*

5 *In a short time she has grasped the concept and is soon able to trot her pony around on a relaxed rein. With nothing to pull against the pony stays in a regular rhythm*

5

Q How can I get my horse used to large vehicles?

You need to build your horse's tolerance to large vehicles gradually, always working at a level just below the point at which he gets scared. It is always helpful if horses can be grazed in fields alongside roads to accustom them to traffic at an early age. Horses that live on farms get used to seeing quad bikes, tractors and lorries coming and going, so the process of desensitising them to traffic happens almost automatically.

Ask a friend with a small horsebox if they could help. Build up your horse's exposure to this vehicle – perhaps let him see it in the yard at first, then in his field. Have the vehicle parked, and lead or ride your horse towards it using the methods described on pp148–9. Once he can deal with this, accustom him to being close to the vehicle when the engine is running. Then have the vehicle moving slowly. Once he is comfortable with this, try a larger vehicle, or something more frightening such as a tractor. You will have to enlist help, and you may have to pay someone to park a tractor in your field, but it is all in a good cause.

CASE STUDY

PERSUADING TOBY TO SLOW DOWN

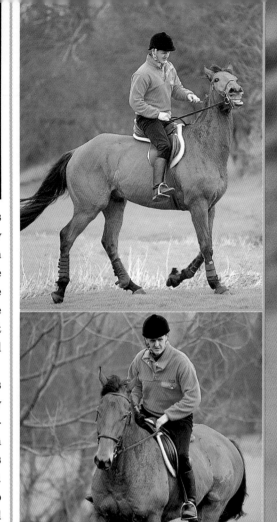

Toby is an ex-racehorse – and like many of his kind he enjoys going fast. However, he is now off the track, and his speedy approach to life is not always ideal. If anyone tries to slow him down his reaction is to put his head in the air. When Mike rode Toby he commented that Toby's mouth was really hard, and the fact that he raised his head simply complicated matters. The root problem was a lack of respect: Toby knew that he did not have to listen to his rider, and saw no point in dropping his head as he had been getting along just fine as he was.

Mike's usual tactic with a horse that holds its head too high is to work the horse on a loose rein and to have his hands slightly lower, on either side of the withers. He has the horse going forward but keeps his hands low to encourage the horse to reach down. However, as Toby's mouth was so hard Mike felt that his usual tactic would just result in Toby going quicker and quicker. Mike felt that he had to keep hold of Toby, but he also wanted to reduce his speed and get him to drop his head. He therefore used lots of turns to slow the horse down, at the same time encouraging Toby to drop his head using the following technique.

Working in trot

- Toby was worked in trot. As Toby is not steady in his head carriage Mike fixed his outside hand on his leg, raised his inside hand and cued with his inside leg at the opportune moment to bring the inside hind leg further under the body.
- Mike kept the bend to the inside and performed lots of circles and turns – when a horse turns he has to drop his head to balance.

Making changes in direction

- As Mike made changes of direction he adjusted his aids so that the new inside hand was raised and the new outside hand dropped down.

Top: *Toby's normal way of going – head up in the air, fighting his rider*

Above: *Mike used the technique described here to encourage Toby to slow down and drop his head*

Right: *To make it easier for a horse to deal with a problem you sometimes have to adjust your position – Mike often takes his weight off the horse's back and rides in a more forward position*

Inset: *Toby is used to carrying his head high so will find it difficult to work correctly – care must be taken not to overdo the work as his muscles will find it hard going. Mike thinks Toby will probably come round to a better way of thinking and going within four or five days. Toby should then have a couple of days off as his muscles will be tired and there is a danger of overtraining*

5 Jumping problems

It is sometimes difficult to remain detached when dealing with problems, especially those that involve riding. Riders often find themselves questioning their own abilities as well as their horse's behaviour. If you are to deal with a problem successfully you first need to sort out your own anxieties on the ground – worries will only magnify once you are in the saddle. Do get appropriate help if your horse's behaviour is giving you cause for concern – often the reassurance of an experienced helper on the ground gives the rider the extra confidence needed.

However, if you have gone beyond the point of being anxious and are actually frightened by your horse you will need to consider your situation seriously. It will be impossible for you to deal with the problem on your own. Fortunately, most people ask for help before they get that frightened. It is always much easier to nip a problem in the bud than to deal with it once it has mushroomed out of all proportion.

Remember the Think Equus principle of awareness of yourself and the horse. If you can adhere to this and work second by second with your horse you will be able to help him without provoking confrontations. Some misguided people like to 'show off their skills' by picking arguments with horses and then showing the animals that they are boss. This may look impressive to the uneducated horse person but to the thinking, caring rider, it is a sign of ignorance. The majority of horses are genuine animals that want to please, and there is no reason why they should receive heavy-handed treatment.

Whenever you hit difficulties run through the Think Equus principles as you consider how to sort out the issue. Using these principles as a basis you can deal with a huge range of problems, and each time you do so your confidence will grow.

Q My horse always rushes at his fences. I thought it was because he enjoyed jumping but I've been told he may be in pain or frightened. How can I tell?

Some horses genuinely want to get 'stuck in' when they see a fence in front of them. However, many horses rush their fences and sadly many owners assume this is because their horses are being enthusiastic, but usually this is far from the truth. A horse may rush for several reasons:

- Pain or discomfort from a physical problem such as a sore back or feet, or dental pain, or from badly fitting tack.
- Fear. This can affect any horse at any age, but is more frequently seen in young horses that have been asked to jump too big, too soon. In this case the necessary education for teaching the horse how to jump has been neglected and he becomes frightened either by the size of the fence or, more commonly, by misjudging the fence and rapping his legs on a pole. The pain associated with this, or even the noise of hitting the fence, causes a horse to see jumping as something to be avoided in the future. So the next time out he does his best to avoid the jump altogether by stopping or running out. If a rider is what is known as 'a strong rider' and capable of getting the horse to jump in spite of his reluctance, the horse eventually will jump but invariably rushes because he wants to get the problem behind him as soon as possible. In this situation it's almost as if a horse closes his eyes and reverts to natural horse behaviour in the face of a problem: which is, of course, to flee.
- Fear can also be caused by an unbalanced rider hanging on to a horse's mouth and causing pain, or a rider gripping with their legs and hands which may feel like tension to a young horse. Bumping on a horse's back on take-off, or more often on landing, or any hindrance by a rider causing a horse to twist and strain as he jumps, will also create a fear of jumping.
- Anxiety in the rider – the rider's emotions are inevitably transmitted to the horse.
- The horse has not been properly trained to jump and finds the whole experience worrying.
- A rider who thinks that speed will help their jumping and who has always ridden the horse into a fence really strongly. Consequently the horse will not know of any other way to approach fences.

The possibility of tack and rider error can be eliminated by loose jumping your horse without tack or rider. If he still rushes his jumps it's likely to be a discomfort/schooling/education/confidence issue. If he is fine without a rider and only rushes fences with one, check your tack and your riding.

CHECK YOUR HORSE'S BODY LANGUAGE FOR SIGNS OF ANXIETY

The horse's appearance will provide clues as to whether he is frightened.

- He will look tight around the mouth, and his eyes will mirror his feelings.
- His ears may well be pointing backwards or constantly flicking backwards and forwards.
- His body posture will be tense rather than relaxed, usually with his head held higher than normal. This uneasy posture can also be seen in a horse suffering from considerable pain – such horses usually jump with hollowed backs and with their legs trailing.

Left: A calm way of going is far preferable to a tug-of-war

Why might he be in pain?

Degrees of pain can vary, as can a horse's tolerance to pain. Some horses refuse to jump at the slightest twinge whereas others carry on, experiencing considerable discomfort until one day they can cope no more.

It certainly helps to know your horse so that you are immediately aware of any small changes in behaviour or way of going – these are often the first

Above: Note any unexpected changes in your horse's behaviour as they may be early clues to a physical problem that is brewing
Right: Horses will rush fences for a number of reasons. You can see here how a raised head and hollow back makes for an uncomfortable jump for both horse and rider

clues that something is not right and that the horse is experiencing discomfort. You should immediately have his tack, back, feet and teeth checked.

A word of warning here. Many people have a scant knowledge of tack fitting and think they are experts. Have your tack checked by a saddle fitter who has attended and passed the Society of Master Saddlers Saddle Fitting course. There are also good saddle fitters who have not yet taken this relatively new course – in either case ask the person concerned to explain what they are doing and why. They should be able to explain what they are finding with your horse, why they are fitting a particular saddle, and how it will help. Some therapists,

such as Equine Muscle Release Therapists, have also had training in saddle fitting. Do not be afraid to question people as to their qualifications.

The whole question of 'back' people is complicated – there are undoubtedly some good people out there who have an understanding of the horse's back and are able to help. There are many more that at best do little to help, and at worst exacerbate your horse's problem. If you suspect your horse has a back problem your first port of call should be your vet. If your vet thinks another person, such as a physiotherapist, could help, he can normally recommend someone. One of the co-authors, Lesley, is an Equine Muscle Release Therapy practitioner, and she and her EMRT colleagues have been able to help many horses in this situation. EMRT practitioners always work with the permission of the attending vet. For more information on this effective therapy see p158.

Good farriery is essential to your horse's welfare. If your horse has an imbalance in his feet this could well result in some discomfort when he is

asked to perform over jumps; the strain taken by the forefeet and legs when landing is considerable.

If a horse has a problem in his mouth the effects can be felt throughout his body, resulting in muscle tension and an impaired way of going. Horses should have their teeth attended to at least once, and preferably twice, a year. Vets will admit that they generally have limited training and equipment when it comes to equine dentistry. A more highly trained and qualified person is therefore needed. Until recently there were very few people available, but now there are two organisations dedicated to improving the situation (see p158).

If you get all these areas checked you should discover the root of your horse's problem. Once the source of pain or discomfort has been removed your horse may need some reschooling in order to get him over the memory of his jumping fears.

SADDLE FITTING

A good saddle fitter will do the following:
- Examine your horse's back thoroughly before trying any saddles.
- See the horse move with and without a rider.
- Treat each horse as an individual. Problems such as arthritis, poor conformation, muscle wastage and poor muscle development will all need to be considered.

You may have to have a saddle made for your horse. In this case template of the withers should be taken, and will reveal any uneven development. All saddles should be tried on your horse without using any padding underneath. The saddle should be tried with a girth, even when the horse is stationary.

Does the saddle fit?

First ensure that the saddle is positioned correctly. It should not be so far forward that it interferes with the movement of the shoulder. If you can fit a hand's width between the horse's elbow and the beginning of the girth, the saddle is positioned well. Now check the following:

- The saddle must clear the horse's spine. When the rider is mounted you should still be able to see a gap from saddle pommel to cantle, with the saddle giving equal clearance either side of the spine.

- The panels of the saddle need to make full contact with the horse's back so that the weight is distributed over as large an area as possible.
- If you can get your hand in between the saddle panel and the horse's back easily then the saddle is not sitting properly.
- There should not be excessive movement in the saddle if it fits well.
- Viewed from the side the saddle should sit level – it should not tilt the rider either backward or forward.
- Run your hand down between the horse's wither and the saddle, ensuring that the length of your fingers is used. You should not feel any tight spots. If you do, the saddle is too narrow. Check both sides. Remember that horses change shape often and will need to have their saddles checked regularly. Listen to your horse – he will be able to move freely in a well-fitting saddle. If he starts to show resistance to being saddled then check the fitting.

How can I persuade my horse to jump in an arena?

You say that she is happy to pop over logs out hacking, but that once in an arena she becomes very lazy; when you bought her you were told she had won money for show jumping, but you think that seems very unlikely!

It is probably the school environment that switches her off because she knows what's coming and has been drilled to boredom in a school in the past. You can check this by setting up a show-jump type fence in a paddock away from the school to see if she jumps it with as much enthusiasm as she would out on a hack. If she does then you know it's the school that's the problem and not the type of jump. Try the following exercise:

■ Take the jumps out of the school and set them up in a large paddock. Position them with lots and lots of space between each jump so that you create what looks more like a small cross-country course, but built from show-jump fences, with large cantering distances between them.

■ Take her randomly around the field and jump whatever happens to be in front of you. Don't plan it too much but try to be as spontaneous as you can.

■ The change of environment will create the enthusiasm she needs but you'll still have her jumping show jumps, which is your objective. You will have broken her association between boredom and show jumps, and replaced it with enthusiasm and show jumps.

■ Over a few sessions close the distances between the jumps until it looks more like a proper show jumping course. A few more sessions and you will be able to return the jumps to the school.

You should also consider the fact that some school surfaces are too deep and a horse may find it too heavy to work on, become tired very quickly and reluctant to work. You could also try taking her to a show. You'll probably find she'll have more life there because there will be so much going on, and the problem may just disappear.

Right: A rider must understand a horse's nature and motivation if a successful partnership is to develop

Q My horse can jump but is very spooky in the ring, shying at anything and everything.

It sounds as if your horse suffers from a lack of experience and a lack of exposure to the world. You are finding it hard to keep his mind on the job of jumping as he is so busy looking around and shying at the many 'monsters' he sees!

You will need to work on his concentration levels when schooling, and also on letting him see more of the world. Do the latter away from the pressure of competition – take him to shows, but just hack him around to get him used to all the sights and sounds. Start with a smaller show and gradually build his tolerance so that he learns to take dogs, children, trailers, other horses and so on in his stride.

You can let him have some fun by going on sponsored rides, or joining a group of friends for a pub or beach ride. Hire a local arena or jumping course. Just get him out and about so that he sees what the world has to offer.

In the meantime, at home or out on hacks, aim to improve his schooling. Your sessions are intended to teach him, help his suppleness and co-ordination, but initially you have to learn to get and keep his attention. This may mean setting him little tasks to engage his brain – such as being led and then ridden over plastic or through a labyrinth of poles, backing up between two poles, and stepping over raised poles or onto a safe, raised platform. These are different schooling exercises designed to encourage him to think and to hold his attention. They can be included with other more usual schooling exercises such as transitions and changes of pace within a pace, circles, serpentines and other school manoeuvres.

Once you have him listening to you start to include some jumping exercises, such as small grids or jumps arranged so that you ride a figure of eight. Grids can give you both plenty to think about; they teach you to keep your horse straight and to ride with plenty of impulsion. Fences arranged in a figure of eight can help you flow on, but you can improve your concentration skills (and your horse's) by reducing the number of strides around the loops and jumping the fences at an angle.

You can introduce stile fences, which are narrower and need an accurate approach; use guide poles either side if necessary to funnel your horse into the jump. Keep the fences small and approach in walk so that your horse has time to realise what he needs to do. Do lots of jumping practice at home (and at venues you can hire), ensuring that you have jumped lots of courses before going to a show again.

Try a smaller quieter show first time out as you want to give your horse the best chance of getting things right. Enter a class that is well within his capabilities and just aim for a smooth, rhythmical, balanced round. Think of it as a schooling round – if you can go in the clear round class you can pop in the odd circle to calm your horse down, or a transition to halt if you need to get his attention.

TO HELP YOU KEEP YOUR HORSE STRAIGHT USE ANY OF THESE IMAGES WHEN YOU ARE RIDING:

- Imagine your reins and legs form either side of a tunnel and your horse has to stay within this.
- Imagine you have eyes not just in your face but at the front of your shoulders, knees and feet. Imagine all your eyes looking straight ahead.
- Keep your focus well ahead of you – look over and beyond each fence. You can practise this at home when going down grids – ask a friend to stand at the end of the grid, holding up different numbers of fingers. You have to give the correct answer every time!

Q We always seem to knock a fence down when show jumping. Do I need to ride with more impulsion?

Before talking about impulsion we need to establish whether you suffer from first- or last-fenceitis! When jumping people often knock down the first or last fence. The first fence problem often occurs because of nerves or the fact that neither horse nor rider have fully engaged their brains and bodies before going through the start line. Last fenceitis is usually down to the fact that the rider thinks he or she is home and dry and fails to ride the last fence properly, perhaps easing the contact or not using their legs.

If you fall into either of these categories then at least you can recognise the problem and do something about it! If your one fence down happens randomly throughout the course it could be due to a lack of impulsion or a hiccup in your or your horse's jumping style. Whatever the cause, the remedy lies in gridwork which has several benefits.

You will need help on the ground when riding grids, otherwise you may have to keep getting on and off to adjust the grid or pick up poles. Ideally, find an instructor with good facilities and experience of using gridwork. The fences do not have to be big, but a line of six small crosspoles, set with a bounce distance (see separate panel) between each fence, is still a challenge to ride correctly. Your objective is to maintain the same rhythm going into the grid, through the grid and coming out of the grid, with the horse's feet coming down in the centre of each distance between the fences.

You will probably find the first few times down the grid quite difficult as you have to learn how to ride your horse and get the correct balance of your aids so that he finds it easy to negotiate the exercise. Your instructor will be able to tell you whether you need to ride more or less strongly into the grid, and with practice you will be able to feel when you have sufficient impulsion and when you are lacking impulsion.

Remember that impulsion is not speed: impulsion is contained energy, which can be released for the required task.

DISTANCES FOR GRIDS AND POLES

Trotting poles
- 4ft (1.2m) for ponies, 4ft 6in (1.4m) for horses

Placing poles
- Trot approach: 8ft (2.4m) for ponies and 9ft (2.75m) for horses
- Canter approach: 16ft (4.8m) for ponies and 18ft (5.5m) for horses

One non-jumping stride between fences
- Trot approach: 16ft (4.8m) for ponies, 18ft (5.5m) for horses
- Canter approach: 21ft (6.4m) for ponies, 24ft (7.3m) for horses

Bounce (no stride between fences)
- Trot approach: 9ft (2.75m) for ponies, 10ft (3m) for horses
- Canter approach: 10ft (3m) for ponies, 11ft (3.4m) for horses

Q I find it hard to keep my horse balanced when jumping.

He's a big horse (17hh) and is a Shire x Thoroughbred. We can cope OK when jumping outside, but in the confines of an arena I find it hard to keep him balanced around the corners. We tend to lose our impulsion. Can you help?

It is always difficult keeping a big horse together, in balance and with sufficient impulsion, when working in a smaller area. The key lies in his flatwork – the more supple, co-ordinated and 'elastic' you can make him, the easier it will be for him to negotiate turns in an indoor arena. You will need to make him more supple both longitudinally (from head to tail) and laterally (from side to side). Exercises such as transitions, from one pace to another, and within a pace, will help with longitudinal suppleness. Try lengthening and shortening your horse's strides – count the number of strides, for example from H to K, when you are in working trot. Then slow the rhythm and try to contain the impulsion so that your horse is taking smaller steps. Count how many strides you can fit in, between the original markers. Next time around, encourage your horse to take longer steps and see how many strides you can count. You can do this exercise in trot and canter. As a variation, count how many canter strides you can do in a 20m circle and then work on increasing and decreasing the number.

Lateral exercises to help include leg yielding, turn on the forehand, turn on the quarters, shoulder-in, renvers and travers. These help you to gain control of your horse's shoulders and hindquarters. In addition you learn to feel each step of your horse's movement and how to influence him.

Specific exercises to help your horse around tight turns in an arena are shown opposite.

An unbalanced horse, travelling too fast, will be unable to negotiate a turn properly and will 'motorbike' around it. This does not feel particularly good – if your horse does this you need to work on his schooling, using exercises to help his suppleness and your control

Set poles out as a guideline, marking out a route from the side of the school, making a right-hand half-15m circle and then inclining back to the track (see diagram). The poles provide a visual aid and help ensure accuracy. Ride this in trot and then canter, aiming to keep each pace balanced and smooth. Use the outside rein to support and contain the shoulders. Make sure that you also set this route out for a left-hand turn and that you practise both reins equally. When your horse finds this easy, try a half-10m circle and incline back to the track

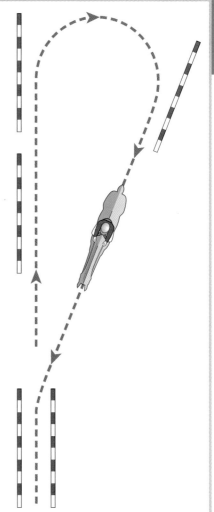

——— Original route,
10–12 strides round loop
Distance A–D: 60ft (18.45m)
Distance B–C: 60ft (18.45m)
——— Short route,
7–9 strides round loop
Distance A–D: 55ft (17m)
Distance B–C: 55ft (17m)

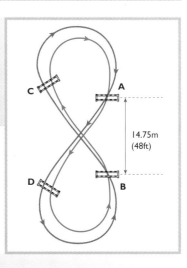

14.75m
(48ft)

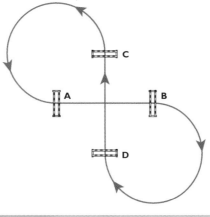

Set yourself a small figure-of-eight course (see above) or a box grid (see left) so that you can practise making turns to fences

Q How can I improve my balance when jumping?

You say you tend to get ahead of your horse, and that if he stops you go over his head. Sometimes riders get so enthusiastic about jumping that they do tend to jump the fence before the horse does! One of the quickest ways to improve your balance is to do lots of gridwork, but in order to gain the most benefit from this there is an exercise you should do on the flat first.

Your balance will be greatly aided if you have a strong lower leg position. Work in an arena with your stirrups at jumping length, and while walking around the school adopt jumping position.

At first you will probably find it hard work to maintain jumping position for one circuit of the school as your leg muscles will soon start to complain. Practise in walk, trot and canter, so that you gradually build up the time and improve your balance. If you find yourself bouncing back into the saddle, use a neckstrap for extra support and just work on getting it right for a short time. Take frequent rests: go from jumping position to normal rising trot and then back again. This exercise will help strengthen your legs and improve your balance. If you find you are constantly struggling and falling out of balance, check your stirrup length. Many people try to jump with stirrups that are far too long.

Once you have this cracked, you can progress to the following exercise. Set up two small crosspoles so that you can stay on a 20m circle and keep popping over the fences. The idea is to ask your horse for a steady, rhythmical, forward-going canter; adopt jumping position and keep going around the 20m circle, taking the fences literally in your stride. You should maintain the jumping position all the way around the circle. Remember to do this exercise on both reins.

You can then make life more testing for yourself by working through simple grids. You will need help from an experienced instructor to set up the lines of fences.

Do not expect to overcome your balance problem in one or two sessions – it will take some practice. You can also ask an instructor to give you some lessons on the lunge to help develop an independent seat.

Top and above: *Compare the rider's position for schooling on the flat to that required for jumping. You can see that the angles of the body are closed considerably at the hips, knees and shoulders in order for the rider to fold and follow the movement of the horse when jumping*

IN THE JUMPING POSITION THE RIDER SHOULD:

- Close the angles of the body.
- Look up and ahead.
- Be able to maintain balance without hanging on to the reins – if you find yourself using the reins to balance, fasten a stirrup leather around the horse's neck so that you can hold this strap for extra security. You will avoid hanging on to the horse's mouth and possibly causing him discomfort.
- Let your weight sink down through your heels, but think of the ankles and heels as being shock absorbers.
- Keep your lower leg wrapped around your horse's sides – think of how a wet cloth drapes itself around an object.
- If you find that your knee acts as a pivot point and your lower leg swings back, think of thrusting your lower legs forward.
- Look at photographs of cross-country riders with good lower leg position, such as Lucinda Green, Mark Todd, Blyth Tait and Andrew Nicholson.

Right: The position and stability of your lower leg position is crucial to the overall security of your jumping seat. If you find that your lower leg swings back, try this: have your feet towards the inside edge of the stirrup iron and at slight angles away from the horse's side (as if your feet were at five to one on a clock face). Think of pushing your lower legs forward as if you are trying to show someone the soles of your boots

Above: When riding you need to be comfortable, so it is important to get the stirrup length right. If you are relatively inexperienced do not try to ride too long – the depth of your seat will take time to develop. As a general rule, your stirrup length will be a decent flatwork length if (from the ground) you can put your hand against the stirrup bar and the iron comes to your armpit. However, if you feel that you are reaching for your stirrups, pop them up a hole. You need to feel secure and comfortable in order to give of your best

Q I have had some bad falls from my horse when jumping and I have lost confidence in him and in myself.

It is very easy to lose confidence and a much longer and more difficult process to regain it. The first step is to be honest with yourself as to the reasons for your falls. Were you trying to jump fences when you were not really ready for the height or type of fence? Did you ask too much of your horse, causing him to stop or jump badly? Are you worried about jumping anyway? Owning up to your real feelings will make the next step easier. If you have tried to do too much, too soon, you can always start again, with the help of a good instructor. If you feel that you do not want to jump any more you need to decide what kind of riding you want to pursue and whether your current horse is suited to this change of direction. You may come to the conclusion that the best thing for all concerned is to sell the horse.

If you decide to go back to basics with your existing horse it is worth remembering that it is the rider's job to get the horse to the fence with sufficient impulsion to jump. The rider should bring the horse to the fence on the best line or approach possible, and both horse and rider should be balanced. It is the horse's job to jump the fence. Working on simple grids and jumping exercises, at a height that does not worry you, will be helpful in re-establishing your confidence and boosting your relationship with your horse.

Q I have an ex-racehorse on loan. He loves jumping but will rush his fences.

Ex-racehorses can be retrained to make excellent all-round competition horses, but this may take a while and an experienced, competent rider is often needed. Racehorses have been encouraged to gallop all their lives, and National Hunt horses do jump fences at great speed. You need to take your ex-racehorse back to basics.

■ See if you can walk, trot and canter over a pole on the ground without him rushing. A horse should be able to do this in a steady rhythm, placing himself at the pole without any interference from a rider. Start with just one pole in walk, and then progress to two or three more randomly placed poles in the school.

- Refrain from trying to hold a horse together, or setting a horse up, or slowing him down. Leave it to him. The responsibility of getting over the pole must remain with the horse. Your part as a trainer/rider has been to make the situation easy enough for him to achieve.
- Start off with simple things, and progress to the next stage when your horse is ready. The objective of each step is to progress to bigger jumps without a horse getting stressed and rushing. You are keeping the horse's mind slow and relaxed through every stage.
- Once this work over a pole is established, set up a low jump of crossed poles. Work over the small fence in walk, trot and canter on a loose rein with the objective of the horse jumping without rushing. As before, do not interfere and try to set the horse up.
- Always think about your horse's mental state and how he's coping. If he finds a crosspole too difficult, make it smaller by increasing the distance between the jump wings until the V-shape of the two poles is lower to the ground.
- Over a few sessions you'll find you'll be able to present your horse to bigger jumps, and he'll keep himself slow because he'll have realised it's much easier this way.
- Each stage should be achievable on a loose rein, completely relaxed and balanced, with no interference.

We must aim to keep horses relaxed and settled from the beginning of their jumping education. It's so much easier to speed a horse up than it is to slow a horse down. Half-halting a horse into a slower pace is not that useful because although this momentarily seems to slow his body down, his mind is still racing. Ex-racehorses in particular tend to get faster if you pull on them. So slow the mind down first and then the body will slow down.

Finally, think carefully before using placing poles as they often only complicate a horse's perception of a jump and may not help at all.

Above left: This horse is strong, and horse and rider have engaged in a pulling battle. Not surprisingly, the horse is winning as he is pulling the rider forward out of position. However, this situation is not satisfactory for the horse – he is uptight, his head is too high in the air, his neck is short and tight, his mouth is open and he is not really able to move properly

Left: By changing the rules a much better picture is achieved within seconds. The martingale is removed and the rider is encouraged to ride with longer reins and a lighter contact. As neither horse nor rider is pulling, the rider is no longer being wrenched forward out of position and she can therefore sit up and ride. The horse is happier too – note the longer neck, lower head carriage, closed and more relaxed mouth and the ears in forward mode. Both can now focus on the task ahead

Q I love cross-country riding but I have a fear of ditches. How can I overcome this?

Quite a few riders are worried by ditches. Fortunately, if a horse has been introduced to them properly, he will not be bothered and will usually make a good job of jumping them. In order to overcome your fear you need to ride a horse that is unfazed by ditches, as you want to concentrate on yourself.

- Start by building a pretend ditch in an arena, using a strip of plastic held down at either side with poles. This is your 'ditch' and you can practise jumping this at all paces.
- Walk up to it first if necessary. Make sure you keep looking well ahead and, if you are worried that your horse will put in a big leap, hold on to a neckstrap for extra security.
- Once you have the feel of jumping this and are able to keep your eyes on the horizon and not transfixed on the ditch, you can progress to the real thing.

Find a cross-country course which has small fences – many now have special nursery courses, which include all types of fence in miniature and are designed to help young horses and novice riders learn about cross-country jumping and riding.

Ensure you have an instructor with you who can help and have your horse jumping from walk if necessary. This should not be a problem if the ditch is a small one. Have lots of regular practice sessions so that you can build your confidence. Once you are happy trotting and cantering over small ditches you can add other elements such as jumping a ditch and then a rail, or jumping trakehners (rail suspended over a ditch). Keep everything small until you are super-confident and then build up gradually.

Another avenue you might like to explore is to go on a Neuro Linguistic Programming (NLP) course – these are becoming increasing popular in the horse world as the tutor can help you overcome mental blocks and anxieties (see Appendices).

Q My young horse has started to run out or refuse at fences.

Some horses will run out at a fence to get out of doing the work, but most of the time there is a genuine reason: the horse runs out because he finds it difficult. It's important to realise that a horse's perception is what counts. You may not consider it to be much of a jump but it's almost certain he does. There is a little exercise Mike does with riders to help them get a feel of what they are asking their horse to do.

- He sets up a little jump about 6in high and asks the rider to dismount.
- He holds the horse and tells the rider to jump the little fence on foot. It's only a few inches high and obviously a bit embarrassing, but the rider flies over it.
- Mike puts the jump up a hole each side and asks the rider to jump it again. She flies over it again and then looks at him as if he's gone a bit mad!
- He continues, and each time she jumps it successfully he tells her how well she's doing and then puts the jump up once again. Usually by the third time people get a bit negative towards Mike and ask him what the hell he's doing. It seems senseless to them because although Mike knows what the lesson is going to be, they don't.
- Other riders take the challenge on and run into each jump with greater enthusiasm.

Left: Sometimes horses refuse because they are not sure what is expected of them, as this young horse demonstrates. Once he realises that this narrow log is to be jumped he does so, but his inexperience shows as he jumps to the left rather than straight

However as the jump gets bigger they eventually lose their nerve and run out at the last minute.

The point here is this: firstly to some horses it may seem complete nonsense to jump a fence when there is a perfectly good way round and so they question you. Secondly, the horse may have been enthusiastic at first, but as the jumps got bigger he simply lost his nerve and couldn't do any more.

The point of this lesson applies to all horses, not just young ones. There may be several other reasons why a horse runs out. For instance, he could be in some discomfort from a variety of sources (see pp90–1). The problem may lie with the rider, possibly freezing in the last few strides or being unbalanced, and so discouraging the horse from jumping.

Many people make the mistake of over-practising things. A horse can learn what is needed very quickly and will see no reason to continue practising, in this case, jumping small fences when he can already do this. Often the excessive practising is more for the rider's benefit than the horse's. There is a fine line between keeping a lesson interesting so that the horse's previous work is consolidated and built upon, and making the whole thing boring. One of the keys of the Think Equus approach is to make the lesson relevant for each individual – so the pace, complexity and presentation of each lesson has to be tailored for each horse. Sometimes, if a horse is not being given enough time to work out what is needed he will throw in the towel, and start to run out as his way of letting you know that he is stressed and needs some help. This is why it is important that you work with each horse second by second, noting how they react to situations and how they cope with the information or tasks you are presenting to them.

Q My mare is a fantastic jumper but she hates water jumps. How can I overcome her fears?

Water poses problems for many horses – possibly because in the past less aware 'trainers' have used methods such as lunge whips and brooms to get horses into water. Usually these episodes have been accompanied by a great deal of shouting and frayed tempers so that the atmosphere has been generally bad. Horses, who are very sensitive creatures, have often gone into water because they are more frightened of the person with the whip. The horse has not made a genuine decision to go into water – and the inevitable result of this is that the problem is very likely to resurface further down the line.

Your mare needs to know that you are there

Below: This rider is making a good job of riding into water – she is focused on the task but is giving her horse plenty of rein so he can balance himself, and she is giving him time. She has set him up for success so she does not need to use a strong urging leg

to help her and that you will not become bad-tempered or irrational. This is difficult as owners are so emotionally attached to their horses that they find it difficult to detach themselves. But you must: you have to remain cool and logical if you are to give your horse the best chance of success. You also have to set up your training session properly to give her the maximum amount of help.

■ Before you try to get your horse into a water jump you need to test her reaction to water. Does she object to having her feet and legs hosed off? If so, tackle this first by gradually building up her tolerance – initially to the hose being near her, then the hose touching her, then water trickling out, and so on.

■ For your first attempt to actually ride into water choose your venue carefully. Check local cross-country courses for water complexes where you can just walk into the water. Try to find one where the slope is not too steep, the water not too deep and the footing is sound.

■ Set aside the whole day for this exercise so that you can truly adopt the attitude of 'I'll give this horse as much time as she needs.'

Above: *It's easier for everyone concerned is a horse is used to accepting contact with water all over his head, neck, body and legs*

- Ride your horse, at walk, up to the water. If she starts to back off halt and let her have a look. Don't chastise her: just ensure she is facing the water and is paying attention to it. If necessary use your legs and rein aids alternately in order to get first one step and then another.
- You may only take one step at a time but this is OK, providing your horse is making the effort to deal with the problem. If she starts gazing into the next county or swinging around with the intention of running away then quietly stop her and get her attention focused back on the job in hand. Reward every positive step she makes with a rub on the neck or a word of praise.
- The objective is to show the horse that this is a problem that she has to deal with. You will help her and support her but she has to make an effort. You will make it easy for her to do the right thing (step into the water) but difficult for her to do the wrong thing – because every time she steps back from the water she is stopped and placed in the best position to progress.
- If your horse stops making an effort and for example, 'plants' herself, then you hassle her more – not by getting angry or whipping her but, for instance, using a soft rope which you flick from side to side across her flanks. This is more of an annoyance than anything hurtful. When the mare goes forward you reward her by ceasing the use of the rope.

It might be that on the first day you can only get her to the water's edge; or you may get her all the way through. If it's the former then you have to come back again, adopt the same approach and build on each session's progress. This may sound long-winded, but the time invested will be minimal compared to the problems involved in having a horse that is always frightened of water.

Q How should I introduce my young horse to jumping?

You need to be sure that your youngster is strong enough, both physically and mentally, before you make extra demands such as jumping. If you do too much too soon you can create more problems in the long term.

As part of their ridden work, youngsters should learn to trot over poles on the ground happily. Scatter these around your arena or paddock so that your horse will meet them as a matter of course and won't be a big deal to him. You need to ensure you can stay balanced without catching him in the mouth if he suddenly balloons over a pole.

Three or four poles can then be placed in a line so that the youngster can trot through them. Pay careful attention to the distances; you don't want to make the youngster's first attempt a worrying occasion.

AND IF HE REFUSES?

Do not get het up if the youngster refuses the jump on the first occasion. Let him have a look and then turn away, approaching the fence in the same manner as before. It is the horse's job to jump and he needs to have the freedom to do this, so you must stay in balance and allow him enough rein so that he can use his head and neck to balance. Keep your leg aids consistent but do not kick – your legs should be used alternately. Using both legs together means that each leg effectively cancels out the other.

If the horse is happy working through trotting poles, off both reins, you can then build a small jump of crossed poles. Some people like to have the horse trotting over a couple of poles and then a small jump, whereas others prefer to have the small jump on its own so that they can see how the young horse deals with this question.

Reward him for jumping, and by all means consolidate the work by popping over the fence from both directions, two or three times. However, be careful not to get over-enthusiastic with your success and practise until you bore the horse! Horses can learn skills very quickly, and often start to object if asked to do the same thing time and again.

Gradually build up the horse's repertoire of fences – moving from crossed poles to small uprights and then small spreads, for example crossed poles in front of an upright pole. You then need to introduce fillers gradually, initially with the fillers placed at a slight angle to the fence so that they guide the horse in to the centre. As the horse becomes happy with the presence of the fillers they can be moved in so that he is actually jumping them. Fences such as gates and walls can also be included – keep the fences small so that the horse can be walked up to them, if necessary. Let your horse have a look at each new variation of fence.

A horse should place his feet in the centre of the distance between each trotting pole if the spacing is correct for his length

Q How can I encourage my horse to be more enthusiastic about jumping?

If you think about the 50/50 partnership deal, your horse could be seen as not keeping his end of the bargain. However, this could be because he has not really bought into the whole deal. It may be that your horse does not really enjoy jumping at all but he does it because you ask him to. If this is the case then actually he is giving you 100 per cent effort!

There are a couple of points you need to consider. When did your horse start to be less enthusiastic? Or has he always been like this? It may be that too much jumping has caused him to be less than ecstatic. Is his jumping experience always the same, for example, always show jumping, visiting show after show? Perhaps he needs a break from the routine of jumping – either by not jumping at all, or reducing the workload, or varying it by going on fun sponsored rides, taking in a few cross-country fences along the way. Notice whether this affects your horse's attitude at all. Other options include pairs classes at hunter trials, team chases or hunting. Usually such activities give a horse more of a zest for jumping.

Q What can I do to stop my horse dangling a foreleg when he jumps?

This is quite a common occurrence. Providing a horse does not have a physical problem, which prevents him using himself properly, you can improve matters through gridwork. Work through grids of crossed poles but have one side of the cross (on the side on which he dangles a foreleg) higher than the other to encourage him to pick up this foreleg.

You can improve a horse's jumping style and make him tidier by using gridwork. For instance, this horse dangles one foreleg. He could be worked through a grid of crossed poles. The cross would be slightly higher on the side where he is not so neat in order to encourage him to use that foreleg more efficiently

Q What's the best way to introduce my horse to jumping drop fences and going down steps?

Start small and start slowly! Choose a cross-country course that has miniature versions of all jumps so that your horse is initially

just stepping down a few inches. You need to build your horse's confidence so in addition to the drop being small he needs time to work out what he is expected to do.

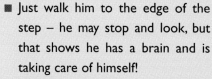

- Just walk him to the edge of the step – he may stop and look, but that shows he has a brain and is taking care of himself!
- Give him enough rein so that he can stretch down.
- When he's had a look ask him to go forwards and ensure that you do not catch him in the mouth. If he does as he's asked let him know he's a good boy.
- If he tries to take a step backwards or sideways rather than go down the drop quietly stop him and re-present him to the step

down. It's the same principle we use whether dealing with a reluctance to go into water, to jump down a step, to load into a lorry or to go forward. You have to keep presenting the horse with the problem and making it easy for him to do the right thing.

- When the horse is happy dealing with this little step you can move to a slightly bigger drop down, and so on. At each stage your horse must be happy. Do not overdo things; there is no point making your horse jump down a 3ft drop, for instance, if you only ever intend to do a minimus cross-country course.

A skill that is useful for cross-country riders to learn is how to slip the reins in case they get left behind. Slipping the reins and giving the horse complete freedom of his head and neck gives him the opportunity to balance himself and extricate himself from a potentially sticky situation.

Above:

1 *This is a sensible approach to jumping down a step. Even experienced horses still need the time to realise what is expected – they just figure it out much quicker than a less experienced horse. The rider is upright to preserve her own balance and is allowing the horse sufficient rein so that he can drop down*
2 *It is important that the rider does not allow her position to creep forward as this could result in her overbalancing and falling off*
3 *The horse is quietly encouraged to negotiate each step*

3 4

1 2

4 As they jump off the last element the rider still has contact with her horse's mouth so that she can control and direct him for the next fence, but there is a good length of rein to allow the horse the freedom to balance himself

Right: This rider has been left behind, but has slipped the rein, giving the horse freedom of his head and neck so that he can balance himself

6 Horse care

People often remark, 'If only horses could talk they could tell us what is wrong with them'. Horses do not speak, as such, but they let us know very clearly when something is wrong – all we have to do is learn to recognise the signs. Awareness of your horse's normal behaviour, and spotting the slightest change the second it happens, is a useful skill – and one that most people have to work hard to develop. Once you are tuned in it enables you to prevent minor hiccups developing into huge issues. Mike deals with many horses who have been trying to tell their owners for a long time that they are not happy – initially the horses were polite, perhaps just pulling a slight face or moving away when, for example, an ill-fitting saddle was brought near them. Their signs went unrecognised, so the horses had to be a little ruder in their comments. They may have been ignored again, or worse still told off for their actions. The horses therefore had no choice but to be even more vociferous, with their actions increasing in intensity. In some cases, horses have resorted to rearing the second people get on them, simply because they are in pain and no one has listened to them, even though they have been saying for months, 'This saddle hurts'.

Part of the Think Equus philosophy is a commitment from each party to work for the common good. It is the owner's responsibility to learn how to understand her horse and then commit to listening to him. Your horse will tell you what he is experiencing – horses are very honest. They have no reason to be anything else.

Q What are a horse's needs?

These are very basic. Social contact with other horses is essential, as is a constant supply of water, and either grass or hay to satisfy their need for trickle feeding. The need to breed is also evident, though this is less pressing – and, of course, only relevant to mares.

Q What is the best way to approach and handle a horse?

It is always important to remember that horses are fragile flight animals. Their instinct is to flee from anything that scares them and even the toughest of horses is surprisingly sensitive. As long as you are aware of this delicate nature and are prepared to be physically and mentally sympathetic, you will be well on the way to achieving the empathy needed to handle them.

Whenever you approach a horse, whether it is in the stable or field, you must avoid aggressive body language. Don't make any sharp movements as this will scare the horse and spark his flight instinct. Instead, make sure the horse can see you approach; never rush, and keep your body language relaxed. Don't spook the horse by suddenly appearing out from behind a bush or popping up at his stable door, but make sure he is aware of your presence as you approach him.

When catching a horse from the field, approach him from the side and give him a gentle rub on the head or neck before popping the headcollar on. Make sure any other horses in the field are also aware of your presence – if you spook one the others will follow –– and lead your horse quietly to the gate.

Adopt the Think Equus approach to leading work each time you handle the horse (see pp14–15), and always be calm and consistent in your handling.

Confidence is an essential element when dealing with horses. Horses are experts at reading body language, and if you are nervous they will sense it immediately. If you are scared you have one of two options: either crack your nerves or give up horses. A horse will sense your fear, wonder what is happening to create this among one of his group and be on edge too. It is a destructive, negative emotion, and one that will hinder your handling of horses.

Top: Horses do need the company of their own kind. Social interaction with other horses is an essential element of their lives – denying this can cause all kinds of problems

Confidence also has a lot to do with your attitude to and respect for horses. Mike has absolute respect for horses and expects this to be a two-way thing.

If a horse bucks violently while Mike is riding him he knows that, providing it isn't a pain related reaction, it is because the horse has learned that this is an effective method of getting his own way. Instead of caving in and dismounting, Mike simply carries on. He takes a few preventative measures – he will try lots of sharp changes of direction to diffuse the situation and take the horse's mind off bucking. Most importantly, however, he refuses to let the horse's behaviour cut the training session short.

As a result, the horse soon learns that bucking is a waste of energy. It gets him nowhere, and his life is actually easier if he listens to Mike and co-operates. This is a good example of how a business-like attitude to a problem overcomes any nerves. You have got a job to do and so has your horse. Your attitude should be, 'You are a horse – horses are ridden out – so deal with it'.

You need to achieve a balance. Horses are herd animals who understand co-operation, so you've got to set down the rules, make it clear what you expect the horse to do and let him make the decision to comply. If he doesn't co-operate, you make his life hard. If he puts the effort in, you reward him by being nice. Remember: it's down to both of you.

ADOPT A BUSINESS-LIKE APPROACH

People often ask how Mike manages to appear so confident around horses, however dangerous their behaviour. To Mike, confidence is all in the mind. Whenever he deals with a horse he deliberately puts himself in a business-like frame of mind and this automatically increases his confidence. He has a job to do and so does the horse. Nerves don't come into it – instead it's a business proposal.

Above: You have an opportunity to strengthen your relationship or, alternatively, weaken it, every time you handle a horse. Be consistent and fair in your handling, always treating your horse with the respect and courtesy you would expect to be shown

Q How can I tell if my horse is thinking?

If a horse is thinking about what you are doing his head will drop, his eyes will go soft and he will start to lick and chew with his mouth. Often his ears will flick forwards and back – which is known in Denmark as the 'working ear'.

If you see your horse doing this you know he has smelt something intriguing – horses have survived by making full use of their senses. When introducing something new to a horse, such as loading, he will sniff the ramp, use his mouth to investigate, test the ramp for safety by pawing it, and so on

Q Do you treat stallions differently to mares and geldings?

The Think Equus principles are the same whether dealing with a stallion, gelding or mare. The difference is that you often have to work at a different level with stallions.

You are still looking for a 50/50 balance, but that might be more challenging to achieve. Often a stallion's behaviour is a bit more full on. Mike likens it to rowdy rugby players in a pub –– all-male bravado and back-slapping. A balanced relationship is still achievable but you have to work harder to gain the equilibrium.

As with all animals, however, stallions vary in their temperament so you can't generalise. Breeding stallions tend to be more hyped up than

most, but you can get some effeminate, sensitive stallions just as you can see tough, tomboy mares.

The basic Think Equus principles apply whatever the horse's sex, but there are also differences in temperament between mares and geldings which call for subtle variations in the way you treat them.

As a general rule, geldings tend to be more straightforward than mares. One gelding is essentially like another in that they are fundamentally uncomplicated. Mares, on the other hand, are more sensitive and moody. Mike actually prefers dealing with them as he likes the fact that they have more complex, complicated personalities.

Rather than setting down one list of rules for mares and another for geldings, it's a case of treating every horse as an individual; empathising with them and adapting your horse care skills to cater for the unique personalities of each one.

Q What tone of voice should you use when dealing with horses?

As a general rule, loud people are bad news as far as horses are concerned. You should always keep your tone of voice quiet yet authoritative.

There is never any need to lose your temper and shout at a horse. He won't understand why you are making a lot of noise and will simply become agitated and worried.

Body language is more important to a horse than words, but when you do use voice commands, make sure they are effective. For example, how many times have you watched someone lunge a horse, saying 'Walk' as the horse trots in a circle? In the horse's mind the association is that 'Walk' means trot. Instead it's important to train yourself to say 'Walk' just at that instant when the horse slips down a gear.

What difference does a horse's age make to how you handle him?

As a general rule, younger horses are more open to new ideas than older ones. They are a bit like humans in that respect. For example, you might come across an elderly horse that has a habit of dragging people down to the paddock. There's a good chance that each trip to the field for the past 20 years has resulted in a battle of wills. Show that horse how to lead properly so he is not getting pulled around and shouted at and you will undoubtedly make his life easier. But the chances are he won't listen. He has charged down to the field every day for 20 years and he likes doing that. Why should he change?

Horses can get become stuck in their ways. You might persuade some to change their attitude, but it stands to reason that an older horse won't be as open to change as a three-year-old.

But that doesn't mean to say that all youngsters are easy to train. Some two- or three-year-olds can be a devil to handle as they have reached the stage where they are becoming curious about life, but are not yet old enough to be ridden. Like boisterous, naughty children they become bored standing in the field all day and look around for things to occupy their mind – be it chewing fences, chasing their fieldmates, or playing up when you go to catch them.

Their behaviour often improves when 'school time' arrives and they start work, but young horses need to learn to respect and listen to us and be polite. They often benefit from leading work and long-reining exercises, which helps to keep their mind occupied. If they learn to be polite at a young age and are reminded of this every time we handle them, there's less chance that they will become bolshy and difficult when they get older.

 ## How can I learn to think like my horse?

Learning to think like a horse is a key element of Think Equus, and to gain an understanding of what makes horses tick you must consider their lifestyle, instincts and priorities in life.

It is tempting to give horses human personalities, but in fact the two species couldn't be further removed from each other. Horses are experts at living in orderly groups, or herds. They have hundreds of thousands of years' experience of living in co-operative groups and working things out among themselves in order to eke out an existence. Being an accepted member of a group is essential for survival. In the wild, lone horses are vulnerable to predators, so they

It is helpful if your horse will allow himself to be touched all over as this makes everyday attention much easier. Horses are very tactile creatures – they will enjoy being scratched or rubbed and may even groom you in return

appreciate that communal living is vital, and that it calls for a bit of give and take.

Humans are the opposite. We may prefer to live in groups of two or more, but being on our own doesn't necessarily mean danger. Horses live in herds because there is safety in numbers. Thousands of years ago humans would have been one of the groups of hunters they feared, so it is a tribute to the equine species' generosity of nature that we manage to co-exist at all.

Horses are very simplistic in the way they deal with field squabbles, which are dealt with quickly and efficiently. An errant horse will be put in his place by other group members, or face expulsion from the herd. Human relationships, meanwhile, are affected by complicated egos and personalities.

It is only when we learn to appreciate these differences that we can begin to empathise with horses and learn to think like they do. Horses have evolved to run away from problems; we have evolved to work problems out. Horses understand complex body language; we are often blind to it. All these differences will create huge problems between horse and rider unless we take time out to understand them. But by studying the way a horse sees life we can help him work through problems and gain his trust and respect.

CHLOE'S FEAR OF THE FARRIER

For Mary-Jane, her 50th birthday celebrations proved to be a life-changing event. After 30 years of focusing on her family and career, Mary-Jane could finally indulge a lifelong ambition to have her own horse.

The search for a perfect equine partner culminated in the arrival of 17.2hh Shire x Thoroughbred, Chloe. As the pair got to know one another, Chloe appeared to be the kind, willing horse Mary-Jane had dreamed of – despite the odd bout of cow-phobia.

An impossible situation

Cracks started to appear in the relationship when a routine visit from the farrier revealed Chloe's utter fear and intolerance of being shod. Mary-Jane had bought Chloe from a riding school and was aware from the outset that she wasn't good to shoe. However, the problem had now become so severe that any attempt to shoe her resulted in sheer panic, with Chloe rearing up and kicking out every time the farrier tried to go near her legs. On one occasion she kicked the farrier's toolbox clean out of the yard. Mary-Jane was convinced that Chloe's behaviour was genuinely due to worry rather than naughtiness and tried to think of ways to find the root of the problem.

Mary-Jane researched Chloe's history and found that her previous owners had tried a variety of things to get Chloe shod but she had still always been difficult to shoe. They even tried starving Chloe for a few hours before the farrier's visit in the hope that a bucket of feed would distract her during shoeing. She was twitched and sedated, but still every farrier's visit involved a huge battle and Chloe just became more and more resentful. Mary-Jane tried everything, but Chloe's behaviour was reaching new and dangerous heights even while sedated.

Things finally reached a head when the vet sedating her said that although she was still conscious, he couldn't give her any more sedative as she had already had over the recommended dose. On top of this the farrier decided he'd had enough, deemed Chloe too dangerous and refused to shoe her ever again. Here was a promising young horse whose fear of being shod was wrecking her chances of a full and happy life. Drastic action was called for, so Mary-Jane contacted Mike and explained the situation.

Mike suggested he should visit Chloe to see what was going on. He worked with her for an hour or so: 'At first she was very sceptical of me and probably thought I was a vet coming to jab her or a farrier to shoe her. She was ready to do battle.

Mike's Solution: 'Chloe was quite a complex character and there was a part of her that was frightened and a part that simply figured, "Well, I don't have to deal with this". For me it was a case of judging when to be sympathetic and when to be assertive with her – always working in the middle ground. The secret lies in being able to read a horse and know what's in his or her head. There were times when she was having real trouble and it was up to me to recognise this and help her with it. On the other hand, there were times when she refused point-blank to even listen to me or put in any effort. It was at these times that I had to tell her to listen and realise the importance of this. Her survival depended on it.

'My first job was to break her preconception of me. I wasn't there to do battle with her. My intention was to show her a way of getting through the rest of her life a bit better. I couldn't imagine anyone ever making a decision to battle with this big 17.2hh Shire cross mare unless they were completely mad.

'I clipped my rope onto her headcollar and just worked in the stable to get her focusing on me and listening, by making lots of smooth changes of direction, stops, starts and a bit of backing up. Once she realised I was on her side I could then be more specific and begin to deal with handling her feet. What most people don't realise is that this is the important stuff: getting a horse to neutral and removing preconceptions first and then beginning the more specific lesson afterwards.'

Mike made a lot of progress in an hour, and by the end of the session was able to tap each foot with a farrier's hammer. He explained that Chloe had done very well but was a long way off a farrier's visit: it was clear that the mare's deep-rooted fears were going to take some more quite specific work to overcome. Mary-Jane agreed to send her to Mike's yard for 10 days.

The farrier came to shoe Chloe there, and Mike showed him what he'd achieved over the past 10 days and how he'd done it. Mike was able to go to each of Chloe's feet, pick them up, rasp round, and simulate nailing on and clinching up. The farrier was amazed at the transformation in Chloe and admitted that until now he had been hugely sceptical of Mike's work.

Now it's hard to comprehend that she ever had a shoeing problem. She's calm, co-operative and shows no signs of nerves. 'The change in her after she came back from Mike's yard was amazing,' says Mary-Jane. 'I couldn't believe it was the same horse. Her shoeing phobia had been a real worry and it was a marvellous relief to watch her happily being shod.'

'The emphasis now is obviously on making sure Chloe never has a bad experience with shoeing again. With any phobia there will always be a remnant of the past. The further into the future you can get without having a problem the less it is remembered and the better a horse will get,' says Mike.

Leading work is always an important part of Mike's training as it gets the horse to neutral before he begins to address any real problems. At the start of a training session this cob benefits from lots of stops and starts and changes of direction. Once he is focused on his owner, she can really begin to work with him.

What guidelines should I work within when handling horses?

There are 10 main guidelines to consider in this respect:

- Partnership: it is vital that both horse and rider work in unison. Neither party should control the other or have the upper hand
- Co-operation and interaction: horses are herd animals. Therefore, the ability to function in a co-operative social group is a key to equine survival. They do it by instinct, but since we don't live in herds it's our role to learn this technique and apply it when we deal with horses – learning to think like them.
- Balance: a 50:50 balance should always be the goal in every horse/rider relationship. This calls for total awareness on both sides and requires constant, subtle changes. If the balance ever shifts in either side's favour, it must be corrected immediately.
- Responsibility: the aim is to create a framework within which each individual is responsible for their own actions. You must expect the horse to put in as much effort as you do.
- Collaboration and trust: as you learn to empathise with your horse you will, in turn, learn to trust him – and him you. This can only serve to strengthen your relationship.
- Diplomacy: battles should be avoided and the cause of any problem addressed, as opposed to turning problems into battles.
- Win, win: rather than treating each situation as a battle you must win, you must ditch your ego and adapt your way of thinking so you achieve a win, win result.
- Setting targets: hope to achieve certain targets, but be prepared to listen to your horse and adapt each goal accordingly. Accept when the horse is really trying and thank him for that.
- The middle ground: when working with a horse you need to find a middle ground, within which the horse will tolerate adjustments to the balance of the relationship. This middle ground should be worked in a positive and creative manner with mutual respect and attention. Work outside of this middle ground and you'll lose regard for each other – and things could become dangerous.
- Dynamic awareness: you must remain aware of the ever-changing nature of yourself and your horse and empathise accordingly. If you leave work in a foul mood, for example, take time out to clear your mind before you work with your horse rather than taking things out on him.

1

Worming

1 *This is the horse's usual response when someone tries to worm him. He does not want to deal with this issue so he raises his head in the air defiantly as this has always worked for him in the past*

5

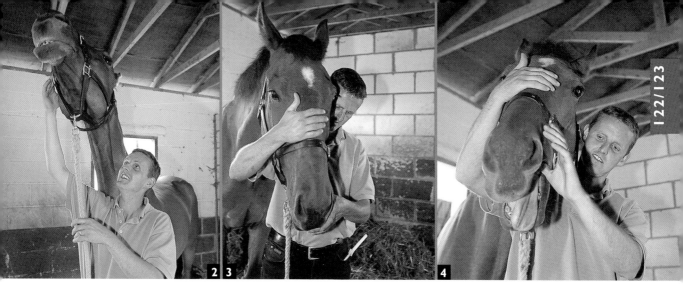

2 To help the horse and himself Mike sets the situation up for success. He works inside a stable but does not try to hold the horse's head down – see how the lead rope is loose, unlike in the first photograph. Mike keeps the worming syringe in his pocket as he has some preparatory work to do. The horse is sceptical – you can see how he immediately raises his head when Mike just tries to touch him with his hand

3 Now the horse has realised that Mike is not like anyone else who tries to administer a wormer. All Mike has done is quietly persist that the horse allows him to stroke his face. The horse has now decided that it's OK to lower his head, and is happy for Mike for continue with some of the other preparatory work. This involves feeling in the horse's mouth

4 The next step is to accustom the horse to the feel of something in the corner of his lips, so Mike quietly puts his thumb there and gives the horse time to get used to this sensation

5 Only at this point does Mike introduce the wormer – and it is a low-key introduction as he continues to work around the horse's mouth while holding the syringe

6 The syringe is then gently inserted into the corner of the mouth – the horse raises his head a little but, unlike on past occasions, is not restrained and so decides that actually he can handle this process after all

7 Success! The worming paste is administered

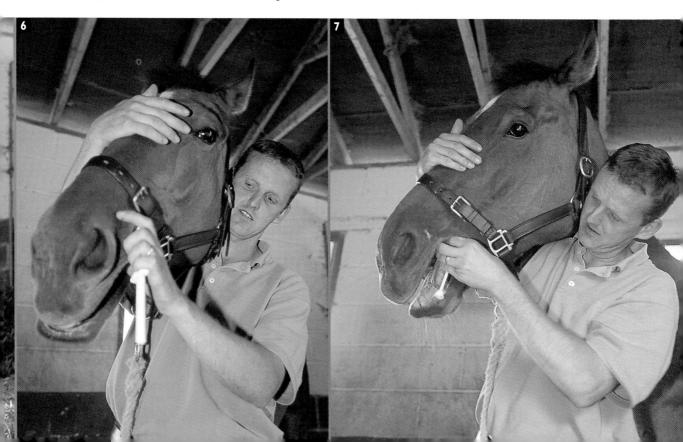

Q My gelding tries to kick out when I try to pick up his back feet.

He doesn't mind me brushing his back legs and my farrier has tried to help but he cannot get my horse to hold his feet up long enough for shoes to be put on.

Horses are naturally sceptical about people handling their feet, and it's something young horses have to learn to trust you with. Mike uses the following procedure:

- First you have to teach your horse to raise each foot on command. Initially he'll lift the foot and instantly put it down again. This is perfectly natural and you should give him a rub on the neck each time to reward him for simply lifting the foot on cue.
- Now ask him to do the same again and repeat the process a few times until he begins to relax for you.
- As he begins to trust you, you'll notice he'll hold the foot in the air for longer each time. This is a natural process and you can reward him by rubbing the leg while it's in the air to encourage him to hold it there for longer.
- After a few sessions he'll get really good at it and you'll be able to hold it long enough for the farrier to do his job.

Be careful not to hold the foot too high, which can unbalance a horse and cause him to lose his confidence in you. Also, if he wants to put the foot down, don't try to hold onto it. This will make him nervous and he'll snatch it away or kick out at you.

Q My farrier used a twitch on my youngster. Is this normal?

The first time my youngster was shod she was well behaved. The second time she became agitated and the farrier insisted on twitching her.

It is quite common for a youngster to be good for the farrier the first time, and then slightly more sceptical the second time when she knows what is happening. Farriers will often resort to twitching a horse if she becomes agitated because they are generally very busy and want to get the job finished as soon as possible. The down side to twitching any horse is that they don't learn to deal with the whole process of shoeing. The twitch causes endorphins to be released into the horse's body which act like a

sedative and make the horse drowsy. The farrier's job is to put shoes on, and while you can expect him to be sympathetic to your horse you have to make sure she is mentally ready to shoe.

You can prepare your horse for the farrier by practising picking up each foot, holding it and simulating rasping round, nailing on, clinching up and so on. When your farrier comes he'll be much happier because he's able to get on with the job, and your horse will be happier because she doesn't need twitching.

Q My horse is scared of the lunge whip. What can I do to help her overcome her fear?

One of the main concepts of the Think Equus philosophy is to only use as little as you need. If your horse moves out onto a circle to lunge in response to you without you having to pick up a lunge whip, you don't need one. If you have to lunge with a lunge whip, use a shorter one without a string or perhaps a schooling whip. Only ever use it to direct her movement, and only ever as little as is necessary to get the required movement forward. Your horse will soon begin to trust that you're not going to hit her with it. When her confidence has returned you can go back to using a standard lunge whip.

It's always good to get young horses used to being touched all over, initially with just the contact of a human hand, then with objects such as whips and plastic bags. You can also build a horse's tolerance so that he is happy to stand without flinching as a lunge whip is draped all over him, or even cracked within his vicinity.

When a horse is young he is more open to new ideas and so can easily be accustomed to strange things like plastic on his back or walking over plastic. This also helps him to use the left half of his brain to work through problems rather than just react instinctively

Q My mare's teats are swollen but she won't let me get close enough to her to examine them properly.

This area is difficult to get to at the best of times, and if her teats are swollen she is going to be even more sensitive about it. Your best course of action would be to call your vet to examine her. If he has problems he'll be able to give her a mild sedative and then examine her properly and treat her accordingly. However, it is always a good policy to teach any horse to accept your touch anywhere on its body. Do this from a young age as it helps enormously if, for instance, a horse needs veterinary attention.

Q What type of vetting do I need when buying a young horse?

There are so many things that can make a horse unsuitable for purchase, and it's advisable to get a full vetting before making a decision to buy a horse, whatever his age. It's also a valid second opinion, and a good experienced horse vet will spot most defects through thorough physical examination. Remember: there is no such thing as a perfect horse and you should bear in mind that even if a vetting finds a defect, you still have the final decision on whether to buy or not. A horse that technically fails his vetting may still be suitable for your purposes. and if you really like a horse don't just write him off and walk away heartbroken but consider everything. For example, a horse's temperament should be considered closely. It would be no good if a horse was A1 physically but your personalities were incompatible.

If you are buying an unbroken young horse, remember he may not have been educated enough to be handled for a full vetting. Whatever vetting you decide on always ask for a blood sample to be taken. This is because there are unscrupulous vendors who will use drugs to mask lameness or quieten a horse down. If you have a blood sample you have the evidence to support your case.

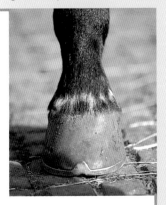

A vetting is a good idea when buying any horse, but use your own eyes as well when you first try a horse. The marks around this horse's leg are likely to have resulted from an injury such as being caught in wire – always find out as much as possible about a horse's history. It may give clues as to what lies behind problems or hang-ups that are evident now

Q How can I keep my horse's outdoor rug on?

She is OK when the weather is cold but as soon as it starts to warm up she removes the rug herself.

With our changeable climate it's particularly difficult to know what rug to put on in the morning when we turn our horses out, especially when the seasons are in transition. Mike always says that if you're in doubt put the lighter rug on. Horses find it much easier to heat themselves up when they're cold than cool themselves down when they are hot, and the worst situation is when they get too hot and sweaty under their rug. Their rugs get damp, and if the weather suddenly turns cold a horse can get a chill. If she removes her rug and then stands there shivering, try a rug with front and back leg straps and a fillet string as these are much more difficult to remove.

Horses need time out at grass, not only to graze but also to indulge in activities like rolling and mutual grooming. Rolling helps to relieve itchy places and removes the hair when the coat is changing. It also acts as a bonding process for the horses living in the herd, as one patch tends to be used for rolling and all the individual smells are combined

My new horse is proving difficult to catch. Do you have a solution?

This horse has a traumatised past and his current owner is keen to help him, but she often cannot get near the horse in the field. The horse did have a field companion but due to injury is now on his own. He has always shown aggression towards people

This is quite a common problem, which usually starts when a horse associates being caught with something he doesn't want to do, like being ridden. The ideal is to have a working relationship where your horse looks forward to your arrival at his field and trots over as soon as he sees you. Obviously he is new to you, and you to him, and it will take some time to establish this relationship. But there is a way of curing his 'Can't catch me' habit.

- Using post-and-rail fencing or electric tape, construct a small stable-sized pen on the edge of your field (about 3.5 x 3.5m/11.5 x 11.5ft).
- When you arrive at the field don't try to catch him, but leave a small bowl of food in the pen. Walk away, leaving him to find it on his own.
- Repeat this process for four or five days without attempting to catch him. Your aim is to break his association with you and being caught, and get him to realise that the pen is the only place in his field that he receives food and that it's a nice place to be.
- After a few days your horse will make his way into the pen as soon as he sees you arrive at the field. Already he will have begun to associate you with good things.
- Do this every day and build it into your daily routine whether you intend to ride him or not. Eventually you will be able to go behind him and close the pen so that he's caught.

Above: Mike spends some time working with the horse in the field, aiming to gain his attention and show that there is a better way to live, without showing aggression and being tricky to catch. As he does not employ the usual methods to catch a horse and is presenting himself in a non-threatening way, Mike creates interest from the horse. Now the horse will approach Mike non-aggressively

Above and right: Mike has the challenge of catching this same pony in a field. The pony's mindset is such that when he sees people in his field he takes a walk in the opposite direction. Mike waits for the pony's natural curiosity to get the better of him – the pony cannot work out why this human is not approaching him, and

Above: Now it's time for the owner to imitate Mike's approach – see how the horse has locked his ear on to the owner. By adapting her body language and changing her approach the owner gets closer to her horse and gets more co-operation than she has been able to achieve previously

However, as this shows, the road to rehabilitating a horse can be a long one! When a horse has been behaving in a particular way for a good while it will take to time to achieve long-lasting results. This horse will need more sessions of similar work in order to progress

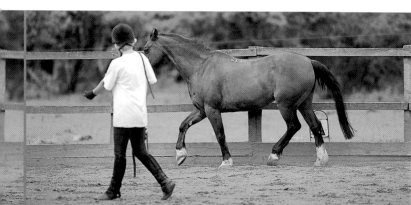

Left: This pony is so practised at avoiding humans that even in an enclosed area such as an arena he will not be caught. As soon as he sees someone coming he clears off. Trying to head the pony off or pursue him does not work – it just increases the speed at which the pony gets out of the way!

eventually he just has to approach Mike…who quietly walks away. Surprised, the pony follows. His behaviour is rewarded as Mike stops and gives him a rub on the head and the pony stands still as Mike reassuringly strokes his neck

The pony has no need to walk away – this person is not playing the game, so neither does the pony. He stands still as the headcollar is put on – note there is no rope or anything to restrain the pony Who would have believed that this angelic pony could be so tricky?!

CASE STUDY

LOADING PROBLEMS FOR OREGON

Anyone who has ever spent an exasperating few hours trying to persuade a reluctant horse to load will appreciate the frustration involved. Whether the problem is due to genuine fear, stubbornness or plain bad manners, the situation can easily spiral into a battle between horse and handler, usually amid cries of 'Use a rope around his legs' or 'Pass me a whip'.

This sad state of affairs is all too common and the result is very often a stressed, unhappy horse and an equally upset handler. However, with patience and the right approach, a problem loader can be dealt with calmly and effectively – as geology student Patrick discovered with his horse, Irish cob gelding Oregon.

Patrick bought Oregon as a four-year-old two years ago, and always had a bit of a battle on his hands when it came to taking him anywhere in the trailer.

A naturally sympathetic horseman, Patrick's approach was always to take his time with Oregon and work on building his confidence. After all, he would always load eventually: it just took time.

One morning the pair were off to a show, and Oregon was having none of it. Patrick was well used to this stubborn streak, and began the by-now regular routine of gently coaxing Oregon into the box. This plan of action had always been effective in the past, but when well-meaning helpers held a long line behind his legs, Oregon panicked, reared up and hit his head on the trailer roof. He bolted off into some trees and in a split second all the trust Patrick had been building up evaporated. The episode shattered Oregon's confidence, and Patrick was back to square one.

Determined to crack the problem, Patrick took Oregon back to basics by practising loading him into the trailer once a week and letting him walk straight off again. This plan worked until someone smacked him on the bum to get him in; Oregon panicked again and bolted a second time. After this the running off became a learned habit that Oregon tried each time he went near a trailer.

Things reached a head when, having managed to get Oregon to a show, Patrick couldn't load him up to get him home again. They had to hack back in the dark. Now Oregon wouldn't load at all and things were desperate. Patrick realised things really needed to change. He knew Mike through having spent some time at his yard on work experience for a couple of months previously, and was convinced Mike was the man to help Oregon recover from his phobia. 'Mike came over to the yard and managed to load Oregon in 25 minutes!' says Patrick.

These photographs show an older horse that has problems loading.

Above: *Using the less stressful Think Equus approach, Mike is simply asking the horse to deal with the issue and the horse is trying – he is testing the ramp to make sure it's OK to step on to it. As his attention is constantly directed towards the inside of the lorry he knows that this is something he has to deal with – the problem will not go away. Every time he makes an effort he is rewarded by Mike and made to feel good.*

Opposite: *Within a short time this horse has made his decision – he does not have any reason to fear going into a lorry, he has investigated it for himself and made a conscious decision to load. Horses, once they have genuinely made decisions for themselves, stick to them!*

Mike's Solution: 'When a horse has learnt to pull away its pointless trying to physically slow them down,' explained Mike. 'I had Oregon on a 5m [15ft] rope, and as expected he did his trick of trying to run off. Each time he attempted this I simply fed him enough rope so he could go where he wanted, and then gently drew him off a circle and back to me without getting into a pulling match with him. When he was back with me I gave him a rub on the head, and within three attempts was able to break this pattern of behaviour. I wasn't pulling on him, so he couldn't pull on me, and when he eventually ended up back with me I reinforced this good behaviour with a rub on his head. It got him thinking that running off didn't achieve anything – he wasn't able to get loose and it all seemed like a waste of energy.

'In reality if a horse wants to get away from you he will. If you look closely at a small cob you can see that they are basically big horses with short legs. This gives them the weight of a big horse with a low centre of gravity – excellent for pulling you, and anything else for that matter.

'Once he was back with me it was a case of focusing his attention back towards the trailer where it should be.'

Eventually Oregon made the decision to walk into the trailer, and Mike spent the next 45 minutes consolidating the process by leading him up and down the ramp until the horse was totally calm and unfazed. Patrick was amazed, and when he had another practice session the following morning Oregon walked straight in the trailer. This change in attitude has prevailed ever since.

'Oregon's loading problem was exacerbated when anyone got rough with him,' says Patrick, 'but Mike's calm, no-nonsense approach really had an effect. Ever since then, Oregon has been fantastic to load and it means I don't have to worry over whether I will actually be able to get him to shows or not.

'I learnt so much just by watching Mike that day, and recently I helped someone at the livery yard to load their horse that was being difficult. They had five people hassling this horse but using Mike's technique I was able to load it in just a few minutes. On the yard now they all call me Patrick Peace!'

Mike sums up the success of Oregon's case: 'Once his attention was back on the trailer, it was a case of asking him to take a step towards it. I'd reward each step he took, and give him a rub on the head. If at any point he wished to step back off the ramp I'd feed him some slack rope before asking him to step forward again. A big mistake people make is to try and hold a horse forward and prevent them from stepping back when they want to. This causes confrontation, and in a pulling contest a horse will always win. If you keep calm and don't get into a fight, the horse will eventually come forward.'

My horse is frightened of being clipped.

Someone has suggested doping him. Do you think this will work? Will it solve the problem or will I always have to sedate my horse for clipping?

Apart from the expense of having the vet come and dope your horse for clipping there are a number of things to be aware of. Firstly when a horse is doped he will not know what is being done to him, and so will not learn to deal with his phobia. Instead of dealing with the cause you are dealing with the symptoms and masking over the problem. As a consequence, you'll have to dope him every time you need to clip him in the future. Secondly, doping can be unreliable and different horses will respond in different ways. With some you may not have enough time to finish the clip and will have to call the vet again. Others, although they may appear to be quiet, will still be capable of lashing out, often without warning.

A better course of action is to use a process

THE ARGUMENT AGAINST TWITCHING

Twitching a horse to get a job done may work on once, but it is likely that he will be much more wary on the next occasion and you then have a fight to get the twitch on. The result is a pointless downward spiral of behaviour, with both horse and handler becoming more upset.

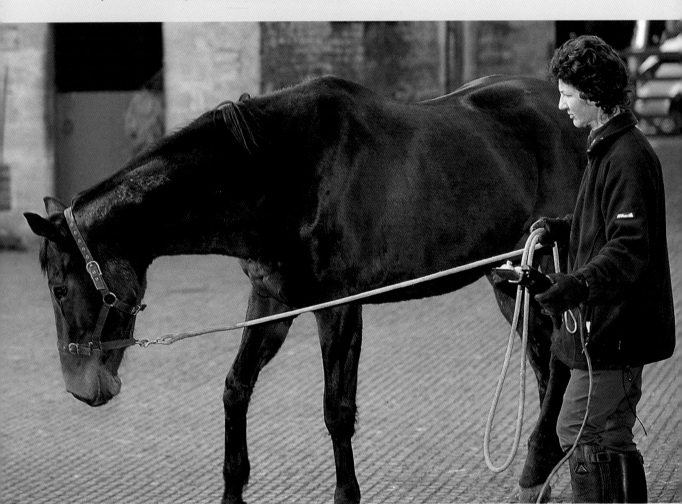

If a horse has never been clipped before, or you have a horse that is frightened of the whole thing, you need to systematically desensitise him to the process. Start with the clippers at a distance from the horse in order to assess his reaction to the noise. As soon as they were switched on this mare moved off

called systematic desensitisation. This makes it possible to school a horse to deal with his phobia in progressive steps. It involves exposing a horse to a small part (duration or sound of clippers) of whatever he is phobic to, and then gradually building up his exposure to it. With your help, he learns to deal with his phobia and he gets to a point of genuine acceptance of, for example, clipping. The help you've given him in overcoming this problem builds his trust in you for other areas of training. Systematic desensitisation absolutely relies on the trainer being able to read their horse perfectly so that they don't overexpose their horse to the clippers at any time. You should never move on to the next step before the horse is absolutely comfortable with the current one.

 ## My horse just ignores me. What can I do?

The Think Equus approach is to immediately ask 'Why?' The reasons can vary with age: for instance, an older horse may try to shut down and carry on with what he's doing because he doesn't want to do what you want. A younger horse may try to blank you because he can't deal with you.

With the older horse you will need to clip a rope on to his headcollar and get his attention; you may have to wiggle the rope to see his reaction or even to gain a reaction. Young horses need a more sympathetic approach.

BE A FRIEND, NOT A PAIN!

Above all, don't nag the horse into paying attention, as this will have the opposite effect. Let him move freely when you are riding; don't hassle him with your legs or hands; and make sure he looks forward to your visits to the stable or field. Visit occasionally just to give him a stroke and a friendly hello and he will start to see you as someone to make friends with.

The problem often arises because people try to do too much around a horse – just think of how everyone gangs up on the poor horse that is worried about loading. Crowding a horse doesn't give the animal the time or space to think or move. If you never give your horse the chance to think for himself then he won't. Either you have to change and adapt the way you handle your horse in order to increase his motivation, or you have to find someone who can motivate and help your horse.

If you are riding, don't kick with both legs simultaneously as this will shut off the horse's movements. Instead use the same principle suggested for young horses: swing your legs and arms in time with the horse's movements, so making it easier for him to carry you and to encourage him to move forward freely.

 ## How much grazing does my horse need?

Generally if you allow 2 acres of grazing per horse you should be able to manage your grassland adequately. This will vary slightly depending on the soil type, field aspect, grass quality, size of horse and the amount of hours he will be out. In winter some heavy (clay) soils will become poached and will be slow to grow in early spring. Lighter soils will poach less and will get growing earlier but may suffer during dry spells.

Horses should be out grazing as much as is practically possible. They love to be outside, but in some cases it may be necessary to limit their grazing. Conditions like laminitis, for example, require restricted grazing particularly in spring. Horses in full training, where the main focus is on fitness, may only get one or two hours out to stretch their legs and to give them a break during the day.

During winter grass quality is greatly reduced and horses living out will need hay and some hard feed while out in the field.

Q My mare hates being saddled, often turning round and trying to bite me.

This is a common habit, and many owners tend to assume that it is just the horse's way and there is nothing that can be done. However, it is often simply a case of the horse communicating that he or she is uncomfortable. Often the problem arises because the saddle is uncomfortable, perhaps causing pressure points if it is too tight or friction from moving around if it is too big. A horse with a saddle problem usually reflects his discomfort in his way of going. You say your horse is lovely to ride, but it might be that she would, for instance, have a much longer stride if her saddle fitted better. The first thing you should do is ask a suitably qualified person to check the saddle.

If all is well, have a look at other areas. For instance, horses that pull themselves along on their forehands, rather than moving correctly from behind, often have sore muscles where the girth fits. Your mare could be objecting because she anticipates pain when the girth is tightened. If muscle soreness or tension is a problem find an EMRT practitioner and ask for their help.

Co-author Lesley has treated many horses with similar problems, using EMRT to help the muscles recover and then teaching the riders how to use the Think Equus riding technique to encourage free forward movement and looseness. This has been used on many horses, from stuffy types to nappy ponies, with success, producing horses that are more forward going, are in self-carriage, and that use their muscles to maximum efficiency.

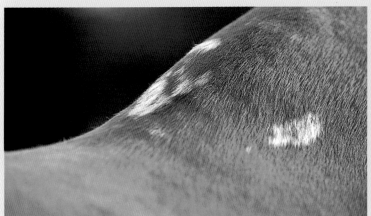

These are classic tell-tale signs of a badly fitting saddle. These white hairs are the final stage of the process that starts with pressure, becomes a sore area, and eventually becomes so deeply bruised that the hair itself changes colour. This shows that the problem was either not noticed or was ignored

Q My 12-year-old gelding rushes off when I lead him anywhere.

Some of the more traditional answers to such a situation would be to lead the horse in a lungeing cavesson or bridle to give you more control. However, these solutions often do not work as they fail to address the root of the problem – the horse's lack of respect for his handler and his established pattern of behaviour.

The point is that if this horse continues in this way he is likely to injure his handler and possibly himself in addition to anyone who gets in his way. This is not acceptable.

You need to go back to basics and teach the horse to show respect and attention by working through the exercise described on pp14–15. Get your horse coming towards you, stopping, turning, and backing up as you request. This will gain his attention and show him that you can manipulate his movement and space (rather than him manipulating you). This work also gets your horse into a more neutral state of mind – at present he acts in a negative, aggressive way towards you.

Once you have gained this level of respect and control in the stable, move on to leading your horse to and from places, such as the field or manège, making stops, changes of direction and so on to keep his attention focused on you.

You can then try it in a larger area such as a school or sectioned-off area of the field. Your gelding should be feeling that the best place to be is with you, as you will have shown him that doing as he's asked is rewarded with praise. Make sure that you use a long rope so that if he tries to pull away you can feed him rope without losing him entirely. Be aware that if he pulls away and you can position yourself at an angle of 45 degrees to him, you can draw his head and hence his body around on to a circle, so slowing him down and changing his direction. If you do this it at least breaks his pattern of 'rush off, get free and do my own thing'!

Left: This relationship does not have a 50/50 balance, for within a short time of leaving the stable this pony is taking charge and pulling away. The handler's attempts to restrain the pony just mean that the pony pulls more and starts to get ahead

The pony's greater strength will always win, and he makes his bid for freedom

Once again this pony's behaviour has brought him rewards

Q How can you tell if a horse has had bad experiences of humans?

When you approach horses, have you noticed how some are friendly and inquisitive while others walk away from you? The signs that a horse is not happy around humans can be more subtle – for instance, he may roll his eye away or tilt his head away, both of which signify that he is thinking about not being with you. Other signs are less subtle – a horse that has bad experiences with people over his feet being handled may just lash out without any consideration for you. Most horses give a warning beforehand, but horses hardened by bad handling feel they have to get their say in first – so they lash out or bite.

You have to assume that most young horses have not been around humans long enough to have had really bad experiences. You would expect youngsters to be sceptical about people handling their feet, for instance, purely because this is instinctive. If older horses are sensitive about particular parts of their body it could be because they have been mistreated, for example hit about the head.

Any negative behaviour, such as trying to bite when you do up the girth, or getting aggressive at feed times, can result from a bad experience with humans. But this doesn't necessarily mean deliberate ill treatment; it

NEGLECT CAUSES EMOTIONAL DAMAGE

Extreme neglect leaves deep emotional and physical scars that can take months and even years to heal. The horse may try to control his fear of humans by being aggressive, working on the premise that he will get in first and protect himself. Some horses will retreat into themselves and become withdrawn and depressed, and will need careful, sympathetic handling if they are ever to trust humans again. Some carry the emotional scars of being mistreated years after the physical signs have disappeared. It is a tribute to a horse's generosity of spirit that they can ever learn to trust humans again, but many do and, with careful handling, go on to enjoy life.

could just be that someone has been sharp and unsympathetic with a horse in the past and he has let it worry him ever since. Horses have good memories and, in very sensitive horses, just one bad experience is enough to stick in their mind and provoke a negative response each time they face a similar situation.

Even the most minor of incidents can lodge in a horse's mind and lead to problems. Maybe someone has been heavy handed with him in the past and jabbed him in the mouth with the bit as they put the bridle on. Maybe the horse has come across something that scared him out on a ride only to be met by an unsympathetic dig in the ribs and a whack with the whip. Horses are incredibly sensitive creatures and it doesn't take much to scar them emotionally.

A horse that is pretty raw and wild and has had no real handling is usually pretty sceptical about people and wary of them, but for different reasons. Wild horses are naturally wary because humans are potential predators.

If your horse raises his head when being bridled or groomed he could either be playing a game or is wary of being roughly treated. Correct him by showing him where you want him to be

Q What does it mean when people say that a horse has 'shut down'?

There is a saying that 'The lights are on but nobody is at home'. Some horses are like this – they have shut down mentally and emotionally and are not letting anyone in. Usually this happens because it is the only way a horse can cope with the abuse he is experiencing. This abuse may be physical but can also be mental and emotional – for instance, horses forced to live alone for years are being deprived of normal stimulation and company. Some horses are just not suited to their current way of life – more sensitive horses, for instance, may shut down if they are used in a riding school.

The eye is a big indicator of how the horse is feeling – 'shut down' horses tend to have a glazed look. Such horses do not respond to you at all – even their bodies are closed, offering no feedback. Normally, interaction with a horse is rather like having a conversation, with both parties contributing. If the conversation is interesting enough you make an effort to listen, even if you are in a very busy place. 'Shut down' horses make no effort to listen so you almost have to startle them into paying attention, by making your lesson more business-like with sharper movements and changes of direction, picking up a foot and so on… anything to switch the horse's brain on. However, remember that you have to work within the Think Equus context so you must always be polite when working the horse. Determining the level of the lesson is a skill that needs to be worked at.

A horse that has shut down is numb in his processes. He has retreated into himself. A horse like this is often described as lazy, but he has just given up on life. He has learned that interaction only ever causes him grief, or it bores him, and so it is easier for him to switch off and ignore everything that is going on around him.

In a way it is similar to depression in humans. A riding school horse, for example, may have spent the last 10 years going round in circles in the school, being kicked in the sides and jabbed in the mouth. Maybe at first he objected to being manhandled this way, but he probably soon realised that was a waste of energy. Nothing changed so he decided to switch off, both mentally and physically.

It takes time to persuade such a horse to take an interest in life again. Initially, Mike just leaves them alone, either in the stable or in the field, to let them be themselves. Often it is hassle from humans that has resulted in this behaviour and they are, quite frankly, sick of us. Then he will pop to see them, give them a quick friendly pat, and leave. Slowly they begin to look forward to his visits, as it's a pleasant experience as opposed to an irritating one.

A 'SHUT-DOWN' HORSE CAN BE ENCOURAGED TO ENJOY HIMSELF

When Mike starts the ridden work with such a horse he tries to literally enthuse him forward. He rides him on a loose rein, doesn't give him any hassle, just lets him find their own pace and rhythm and get used to not being jabbed in the mouth or kicked in the side. It may take time, but eventually the horse's mood will lift and he will start to take an interest in his surroundings again. He will begin to open up and come out of himself, and that is very rewarding to witness.

Q How do I get myself into the right frame of mind for working a horse?

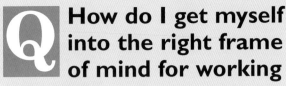

You have to talk yourself into the right frame of mind so you are calm and can focus on the job in hand without outside distractions popping into your head. Your breathing should be deep, rhythmical and easy. Self-talk is a powerful tool – so make sure the voice inside your head tells you positive things and expresses everything in a positive way.

You know that you have all the time you need and that you will get the job done. You are clear about what you are going to do and how you will deal with any hiccups that might occur. You are not putting undue pressure on yourself or your horse because you know you are both ready for this next task. You know you can work second by second so you can anticipate your horse's next move and you will be ready to help him.

When Mike works with a horse he deliberately does not get angry or flustered, nor shouts nor loses his temper – such behaviour would only confuse the horse. Instead he stays calm and keeps the rules consistent.

If a horse wants to call Mike's bluff and back down a ditch for example, he lets him do this. The horse is expecting Mike to chicken out at the last minute as every other rider he has experienced in the past has. When he susses that Mike is as bloody minded as he is it acts as a wake-up call. He thinks, 'This guy's a lunatic – my normal behaviour isn't going to cut short the ride like it usually does'.

MIKE'S APPROACH TO DIFFICULT HORSES

If Mike is dealing with a horse that has such severe psychological problems he is totally unmanageable; he might be the animal's last hope. In a situation like this Mike is basically saying, 'This is it: no one loves you so this is your last chance. All I am asking is for you to listen to me and co-operate. If you put the effort in I will make things as easy as possible for you and we will get along fine. If you don't, I won't. But at the end of the day this has to be done, as there's no place in the world for a horse like you.'

By using this cold approach Mike makes it easier for the horse to grasp the situation. He does not confuse the issue by being too angry or lovey dovey; he merely states the facts. Then it is up to the horse to decide whether or not to co-operate. Mike's philosophy is all about achieving and maintaining an equal balance – which calls for constant, minute adjustments. Keeping the relationship matter-of-fact like this makes an even balance far easier to achieve.

Rarely does it reach the stage where the horse will go back down that ditch. He knows exactly where the edge is and has no more intention of falling than Mike has. Mike is not saying you should try this approach at home, however. He knows just how far to push a horse, but it is a delicate balance.

In Mike's experience, however, it's all a matter of levels. Some people are perfectly happy with their horse despite the fact that he is ill mannered, throws in the odd buck or won't stand still to be mounted. They make compromises and manage their problems and, as long as they're happy, that's fine.

- Remember, horses are masters at reading body language. They are experts at living in groups and can read the tiniest of signals. If you are very positive in your actions and make it clear exactly what you want your horse to do, this will help to cement your relationship and build respect.

- If you have just left work and are whizzing along the dual carriageway on the way to the stables, take a few minutes to prepare yourself mentally before you handle or ride your horse. If you are in a different mood each time you visit him he will soon get confused. So turn the radio on, chill out mentally and leave work, children or partner worries behind.

- If you are tackling a particular problem, be very clear about what you want to achieve and give your horse concise instructions.

- Always motivate your horse to work well. This doesn't mean walking round with pockets full of treats: instead, let him know when he has done well with a gentle pat and let that be his reward. Horses are social animals, remember, so a genuine rub on the head is as effective a reward as a sugar cube.

- Remember, being a good manager translates from humans to horses, so think about the way you are behaving. If you treated your workmates in the same manner you do your horse, would they get annoyed?

- In an ideal world it would be great to operate a reward-only approach to training, but in real life this doesn't work. There needs to be a balance between positive, reward-based training (giving the horse a stroke to say thank you) and negative association training (pushing a horse back out of your space when he pushes into yours, for example). As long as you never bully a horse and always strive for a 50/50 balance, correcting a horse is perfectly natural to him and mirrors the behaviour he would expect to see from other horses in a herd.

- Respect your horse and expect him to respect you, but remember that respect has to be earned.

- Gain as much knowledge as you can about the way a horse thinks and behaves, so you can understand his actions. Read books, play videos or watch a Think Equus demonstration.

- It is a fact of life that horses prefer the company of other horses as opposed to people. Try to work your horse in an environment away from his friends where possible so there is a better chance of gaining, and then keeping, his attention.

- Horses are logical creatures, so always apply logic to a situation, and use your common sense wherever possible

- If you need help concentrating your mind and remaining business-like, consider your horse's workload versus yours. He gets the life of Riley in return for a few hours' work, so it's only right that he listens to you and co-operates.

- Make every training session as interesting and upbeat as possible for the horse and keep the pace of the lesson moving forwards all the time.

- Try to end every training session on a high note and make each goal easily attainable. Lots of tiny minor achievements are far more effective than one, damaging failure.

Q My horse rears if I try to restrain him when leading him to the field. What can I do?

Leading is a key area of the Think Equus philosophy as it acts as a window onto the state of the relationship between horse and rider. By watching someone lead their horse Mike can tell who is in charge, whether or not the horse respects his handler, and which areas they need to work on.

In this case the balance of the relationship has shifted alarmingly and lies 90/10 in the horse's favour. You need to work on restoring the 50/50 balance. Focus on the leading work in general, not just when you lead to the field.

Ideally, leading work should be done in a safe environment at first, like a manège or enclosed field.

■ Work the horse in a headcollar on a long rope and always position yourself out in front. When working with young or problem horses this is the safest place to be should they rear or barge you, and it also gives them an idea of which direction they should be going in next.

■ Make several changes of direction to maintain the horse's attention and keep the pace active so that he has to work with you rather than dawdle along. You want to make sure that the horse is concentrating on you, so that when you stop he stops. He should be watching and anticipating your next move.

■ If he isn't paying attention and barges into you when you stop, wave the rope at him to back him off, give him a rub on the head to say well done once he is the correct distance away, and then carry on.

■ It is important not to let the horse move you once you have stopped. You should make it the horse's responsibility to stop in time. The aim of this exercise is to get the horse thinking about where you are and teach him to be respectful of your personal space. He should be as aware of you as you are of him.

■ Every time you stop, stand your ground. Back the horse off if he has crowded you, and be pedantic. You must make your intentions clear and be deliberate in your actions, both when you are leading the horse and when you are pushing him back out of your space.

■ Make definite changes of direction – your horse is perfectly capable of tight turns – and correct him the second he makes a mistake. As you turn, be clear in your mind which direction you are going to head in. If the horse is in your way, correct him and don't allow him to dictate where you go. Horses are very good at manipulating our movements and if they think they can push you back they will, so be aware of this.

■ If at any point you feel crowded or uncomfortable, stop, back the horse up and carry on. Be fussy and don't let him shift an inch unless you've asked him to.

Mike always expects to be disappointed when doing this exercise, so he is in the right frame of mind to correct the horse the instant he falters as he is anticipating it. If the horse does co-operate Mike says 'Thanks' with a little rub on the head or neck. But don't overdo the fuss; your attitude should be, 'Horses have to be led, so deal with it'.

It is important to keep the rules simple so the horse understands the exercise and learns to think about his actions. Say, 'Push into my space and I will correct you backwards. Be polite and I will leave you alone. Be rude and I'll correct you back again'. The horse will soon learn that his life is easier if he listens to you.

If you are consistent your horse will understand what is expected of him and start to think for himself. This is a great exercise for horses of all ages and levels of experience and it serves as a reminder that we are there to be listened to – not simply pushed out of the way.

The principles behind leading work should be applied every time you handle your horse. Here are some points to remember whenever you are dealing with a horse from the ground:

■ Don't nag with the rope while you are leading, as you will annoy the horse. Keep the rope slack and

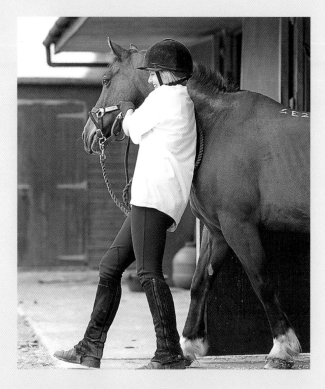

 ## What should I do when things go wrong?

Everyone experiences things going wrong. Horsemanship is not an easy road to travel – you can expect to fall off, make mistakes and learn things the hard way. This is part of normal life for a horse person. Remember too that it is not a right to own and ride a horse, but a privilege. A horse is not like a new stereo or car that you can just expect to work; a horse is a living being in its own right with its own mind and view of the world. Developing a relationship with a horse takes time and effort from the owner.

You need to recognise your own limitations and take responsibility for finding the answer to the problem, rather than doing what so many people do: blame the horse.

When things do go wrong, seek help – but be clever about who you ask. Lots of people will give cheap advice – and often it's free (just think of all the 'helpful' people who will shout at and hit your horse to get him in a lorry!). The people who tell you and everyone else how much they know and who enjoy beating up horses are definitely to be avoided. You can spend your lifetime learning about horses and still know very little, so be very wary of the know-alls. If you have a particular problem, read up on the matter to get ideas on how to overcome the issue. Try everything you can to solve the problem and gain as much information as possible to give yourself the best chance of making an informed decision.

Be aware of your own instincts and feelings – not just in relation to who you let deal with your horse but also in relation to your true feelings about your horse. If you are afraid of your horse or just do not care about him any more then it's time to cut your losses and get out.

Be honest with yourself – you have a responsibility to yourself and to your horse.

make sure he learns to respect your space, just as he would other horses in a herd.

■ Pick up the pace so the horse has to work with you. Remember: the need for personal space is a basic law of nature, so it's up to the horse not to crowd you.

■ Your horse must learn to be aware of you just as you are of him every second you spend together.

■ If a horse is barging you and you shove him away that is acceptable to him. It's what other horses in a herd would do if he got in their way. If you sting a horse with a whip, however, that's not acceptable. That's personal and you will start to lose his trust and respect.

If you spend time re-establishing a harmonious relationship through leading work, the rearing should improve. Make sure you are always positioned out in front of the horse as mentioned earlier. Make lots of changes of direction to keep the horse's brain occupied and take his mind off rearing and, if ever your horse does try to rear, pull his head towards you to regain his attention and don't let the training session stop for a second. Once he has realised that rearing has no effective result, he will learn that it is a waste of time and energy.

Q My unbroken filly has started to plunge and rear in the field.

We had been getting along fine but then she started to rear and plunge when being led to the field. She almost came down on top of me and I am now scared of her. I asked a local event rider for help and they had the filly for a few weeks. She was impeccably behaved for them but now she's home I still have the same problem. What can I do?

You have been honest enough to admit that you are scared of your horse – and your horse clearly knows it. She is using this to her advantage and misbehaving with you but not with more experienced people. When someone is scared of their horse it is best for all concerned if the horse is sold. There is absolutely no place for fear around any horse: it will lead to accidents, and takes all the fun out of horse owning and riding. Horses are an expensive hobby and it is amazing how much time and effort some people are prepared to put into their horses when, essentially, they are scared stiff of them.

If you are genuinely fearful of a horse then it is time to get out. If you feel it is a problem you can work on, you need to make yourself mentally stronger. Mike finds that a business-like attitude to working with horses overcomes any nerves. You may find this approach helps, but being scared is a dangerous and negative emotion to experience around horses.

Horses are sensitive animals and if they sense that you are nervous or scared they will respond in one of two ways. Either the horse will use your nerves to manipulate you and push you around, or he will see it as a threat. He will sense that you are showing signs of fear and wonder what is causing this upset among one of his group. If one horse in a herd takes off in fright the rest will follow instinctively. By showing fear you will put the horse on his guard, as he'll be expecting a horse-eating monster to leap out at any moment.

Above: This horse's usual behaviour is to tell people he does not want any contact by being aggressive towards them. You can see how his ears are pinned back, his mouth is tight and his nose is being thrust at Mike

The horse's threat, however, does not have any impact on Mike who stands his ground. This tells the horse that this person is different – you can see the horse's reaction as he becomes interested in this unusual development. His mouth has relaxed and his ears are now forward, showing where his attention lies

Now there's even better news for the horse as Mike rewards his interested and non-aggressive behaviour with a rub between the eyes

Above: *The next step is to move into the stable. The horse moves away, but shows his feelings by flattening his ears again*

Mike feels that this horse just behaves in a threatening way so that he can be left alone. He does not try to pursue the horse but waits quietly, observing the horse's behaviour. When the horse shows a flicker of interest Mike meets him half way by offering the palm of his hand in a non-aggressive manner

The horse approaches, without showing any aggression, and Mike rewards him by rubbing him on the head

Q My horse lunges at me in the stable and I am not sure how to deal with her.

Your horse could be behaving in this way for several reasons. If the horse is new to you her lungeing could be displacement behaviour: she may be being bullied by the other horses, but is taking it out on you. It could be that she is very territorial about her space and is protecting her area. On the other hand, she may have been abused in her stable and feels the only way to exist is to get the first punch in! The stable, and the food contained within it, are not your horse's property, despite what she may think. It belongs to you both. It is perfectly natural for a horse to be possessive over her bowl of feed, especially if she has ever been left to go hungry on a regular basis. However, your horse has to realise that there are space issues here – you are entitled to your personal space, and she is entitled to her space.

It is your job to bring the relationship back to a 50/50 balance. To do this you need to make very clear rules, while at the same time communicating to the horse that her life will actually be more enjoyable if she accepts the rules and co-operates.

- As you approach her stable take note of what she does. Don't just walk into her stable; stand at the door, offer the back of your hand and watch her reactions. It's likely that her behaviour has either backed people off or made them more aggressive towards her. You need to show her that the behaviour will not provoke either reaction from you.
- You need to open up the space between you and your horse so she doesn't feel threatened or annoyed. If she is very aggressive, take a coiled up rope into the stable and use it to back her off gently when she comes at you. Don't allow her to push you back. Stand your ground and move her out of your space. Draw an imaginary line dividing your space and her's and don't let her cross it. Then, once she is a polite distance away, leave her alone and say thank you.
- Make her motivation to co-operate with this exercise clear – if she opens up the space between you, you leave her alone and her life is made easier.

Then you can slip on a headcollar and rope and get some respect and attention by using the exercise described on pp14–15. This will also help change her mindset, and show her that you are prepared to help her if she will also contribute to the relationship and work towards a 50/50 partnership.

How can I prevent my horse from windsucking?

There are a couple of different types of collar that have been designed to make it uncomfortable for a horse to grab hold of something and then take in air, but these do not really help the horse. A horse may start to windsuck for various reasons, but often a management problem lies at the root of the matter.

A horse is naturally supposed to roam large areas of land in company with other horses, eating for 16 hours out of every 24. As he grazes, he chews an incredible 30,000 times per day. Most domesticated horses do not get that much time at liberty, and certainly not over large tracts of land. If left in small paddocks where there is little to eat, or confined to stables for long periods without ad lib hay, the horse has a problem. His whole body is programmed to chew but he has nothing to chew! So he starts to look for other ways of occupying his mouth and his time, and stereotypical behaviours such as windsucking start.

There is still a misplaced belief that such behaviours will be copied by horses stabled within sight of the 'problem' horse. However, research has shown that the best way to deal with stereotypical behaviours is to give the horse more roughage more often, turn him out more, allow him more interaction with other horses, and bed him on straw in preference to shavings.

A HUMAN SOLUTION

Mike believes that stress and excess acid in the gut contribute to a horse's windsucking. A few years ago he had a confirmed windsucker in his yard and was considering what to do. Humans simply take a pill to neutralise any excess acid – so Mike gave the horse six indigestion tablets before he was fed. Previously the horse would grab some feed and then windsuck, grab more feed and then windsuck, and so on. After the horse had the tablets he stood happily and ate his feed. Once he had finished he did windsuck, but far less frequently than before.

A committed windsucker will even practise his habit when turned out. Note that this horse's headcollar is fitted too low, and it is advisable to use a leather headcollar which would break in an emergency

When I go to shows my horse rears, bucks and kicks out.

The excitement of a show can sometimes be too much for a horse to deal with, particularly if the horse is young. It sounds like your horse is suffering from a lack of confidence in what she perceives to be a hostile environment, hence her apparent change in temperament.

Find a small show locally with not too much going on. This will take the pressure off both of you, and eventually you'll be able to progress to bigger events as she becomes more confident. Alternatively arrange to ride with small groups of friends at home, and simulate a small show in a controlled environment, where other horses trot, canter and jump around her. Spend time developing her now and you'll have a good horse in the future. It's very easy to rush this process and blow a horse's mind. Rectifying the situation is a very long and slow procedure.

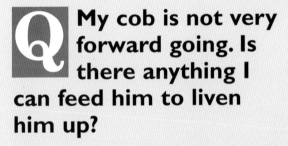 **My cob is not very forward going. Is there anything I can feed him to liven him up?**

Before changing your horse's feed consider some of the other reasons he may have for not wanting to go forward.
- Is he unfit and finding it too hard to keep going?
- Is he bored and lacking motivation?
- Is it a physical problem – does he suffer from joint or back stiffness, or (more commonly) is a rider restricting his natural movement?
- Lethargy is a symptom of depression – is he depressed?

If you are happy that none of these reasons apply to your cob then talk to an equine nutritionist for specific advice – see the panel of contact numbers on p158.

 What can I do to encourage my mare to eat?

This is quite a common problem, especially in horses that are stressed or highly strung. A change of feed often helps, but only until the novelty of the new feed wears off. Horses are trickle feeders and have evolved in a way that requires them to spend the majority of their day eating. Try splitting the mare's hard food ration into smaller portions and feeding her in mini meals throughout the day.

If this doesn't work, consider this. Horses are not designed to eat cereal feeds, and though it may not be a popular view, it may be necessary for you to cut out her hard feed altogether and find natural alternative ways of feeding. Look into different forage alternatives that have a similar nutritional value as the coarse mix you've been using. Perhaps good quality hay and alfalfa mix with a vitamin and mineral supplement lick would be an alternative.

It's possible to get toys that release food as a horse plays with them in the stable. Mike is not keen on these because they make a horse work for food, which is unnatural and can actually cause them frustration. Unlike predators, grazing animals rarely have to hunt and work for food.

Ultimately try to find out why she doesn't want to eat. If it is stress, make the necessary changes to her routine, training or management.

Q How can I persuade my horse to lift his feet up?

It is common for horses to either lean on you when you pick their feet up, try to evade by walking off before you have a chance to get near their feet, or simply refuse to co-operate at all.

If Mike is dealing with a horse that dislikes people handling his legs he does some leading work first to get the horse concentrating on him. Then, still using the long rope, he runs his hands down each of the horse's legs.

A long rope is essential as it enables Mike to stay with the horse even if he tries to shuffle away. His method is simple: if the horse moves, he moves until they have reached the stage where the horse realises that trying to get away is a waste of his energy and it is easier for him to stand still. From there things usually progress pretty swiftly and the horse allows Mike to touch each leg and then, eventually, pick the foot up. Mike makes the rules simple, asks the horse clearly to lift his foot, and then leaves it up to him to co-operate.

Ideally you should aim to get to the point where you cue the foot up and then the horse holds it up himself. It is not your responsibility to hold the foot; the horse has got to put that effort in. Remember too to always touch the outside of the leg when teaching a horse to pick his feet up. This way there is less chance of you getting injured should he kick out.

You should also consider how the horse is standing; it is unfair to ask him to stand on three legs unless he is standing square. Make sure he is, then cue the foot up by touching the fetlock and, once the horse has lifted his foot, hold it lightly for a couple of seconds before letting him drop it again.

Let the horse know that you are pleased with him every time he lifts his foot correctly, and gradually extend the amount of time the foot is off the ground until the horse accepts that it is his job to lift his foot up. Keep each session short – 10 to 15 minutes – and always end on a high note. The horse will go away and think about what he's learned, so you can build on this knowledge the next time.

A horse is showing incredible trust by allowing you to pick up his feet. You have to build this trust — make things easy for your horse by having him standing in balance before you ask him to lift a foot, and initially just have the foot a little way off the ground

Horses can get very attached to each other and if separated will become very unsettled, trotting or cantering along field boundaries in a nervous manner

What can I do if my horse won't let me put his bridle on?

It is incredibly frustrating if your horse won't open his mouth for the bit, throwing his head up in the air instead. You need to teach your horse to accept the bit quietly, but obviously this will take time and patience.

- Stand to the side of your horse's head, let the reins drop on the floor, and hold the headpiece between thumb and forefinger so there is less leather dangling in front of the horse's eyes.
- Stand quietly like this for as long as it takes. When the horse starts to drop his head, hold the bit below his mouth so that eventually he will learn to feel for it himself.
- Reward the horse's decision to drop his head by taking the bridle away for a couple of seconds. Then try again, nudging the horse's head to and fro to encourage him to relax if necessary.

Every time the horse accepts the bit, take the bridle away again momentarily as a reward rather than hook it over his ears. It will take time to encourage a seasoned teeth-clencher to accept the bit happily, but this technique will work if you give it time.

What are the signs of separation anxiety in a horse?

My horse is kept on a nearby farm and the only other horse on the yard has just moved away. Since then my horse has been trotting up and down the fence in his field. He will not settle. What can I do?

Horses do form very close friendships with other horses, and if these partnerships are suddenly split up both horses can feel a great deal of distress. If you had known that the other horse was going to be moved you could have started to separate the two horses, building up the time they were apart, in preparation. Now all you can do is ease your horse's distress. Is it possible to put him with other horses so that he has a chance to form other friendships? This might mean moving him to a larger yard or trying to find someone else with some horses to join you at the farm. In the meantime, spend as much time with him as you can. You could also try giving him Bach Rescue Remedy – add 10 drops to his water or to his feed. This has been found to be helpful for horses suffering from a sense of loss.

How do I stop my horse biting me?

A young horse will often nip and bite and, if he gets a reaction, will see it as a game. To avoid this, lead the horse using a long rope and position yourself out in front so he can't actually reach you to bite. Once he has realised that he can't nibble he will stop trying. Increasing the pace of the leading lesson may help too, as by keeping a young horse's mind occupied he will be less inclined to mess around.

Young horses will often test people out, and nip. They have to be shown that respect for space applies to humans as well as other horses

If you are dealing with an older horse that lunges at you when you pass his stable, ignore him. If you need to go into his stable, back him up, waving a coiled up rope at him if necessary, and, once he is out of your space, leave him alone.

Don't go into the stable with an aggressive attitude as the violence will merely escalate and the horse will have a legitimate reason to take offence. Instead, let it be known that you are uncomfortable with his behaviour and need him to respect your space.

Q How can I persuade my mare to load every time?

I have a lovely mare but she has one problem – she will not load very easily. Sometimes, with a lot of persuasion, we can get her in but she is not reliable so I cannot go to shows and so on.

It goes against a horse's nature to enter a dark confined space from which he can see no escape. Yet this is what we expect: and when the horse says 'Hang on, I want to think about this first', most people get really irate and start shouting, hitting him with whips, brushes, lunge lines and so on. Not surprisingly, a horse that was doubtful about loading soon decides that his initial suspicions were well founded!

Traditional advice on loading also includes things like parking the vehicle against the wall to reduce the number of escape routes for the horse, or getting crossed lunge lines behind him so that he cannot go backwards very easily. This does work with some horses, but even so, the animals have only loaded because they have no other option or no longer feel able to fight back – they have not made a decision themselves that loading into a trailer or a lorry is OK. These horses may well resort to arguing about loading in future, and may even become worse with each loading incident, requiring their handlers to adopt even more bizarre and brutal ways to get them into the trailer.

However, when a horse makes a conscious decision to do something he will stick with it in the future, because no one has coerced him; he has faced the dilemma, thought it through, and come to his own decision. This is what we want.

It is perfectly possible to achieve this, even with horses that have a reputation for being bad loaders. The problem is that most people do not give horses the time they need to make the decision themselves. You can see this at any show: a horse is presented at the bottom of the ramp, and if he doesn't walk straight up someone is soon behind him, waving a whip while someone else tries to drag the poor animal into the dark space.

Before attempting to load you should ensure you have your horse's respect and attention – use the leading exercise described on pp14–15. This will get him into a neutral mindset and will show him that you are on his side. The trailer should be as inviting as possible – avoid using ramp gates if possible as if the horse does leap off the side you can get your lead rope caught up in these. Use a long lead rope, and get yourself into the mindset that you will get the job done and that you will give the horse the time it takes.

- Check that you have the horse's attention and then lead the horse towards the ramp.
- Ensure that your body position does not block the horse's forward

This is a common approach to loading: the horse is being held very tightly so he is more anxious and feels more threatened. His head is in the air and he is uptight. As he hesitates someone gets behind him to encourage him forward. The common result of such an approach: the horse does not want to go in and leaps to one side, almost

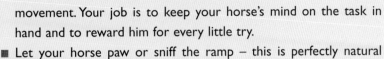

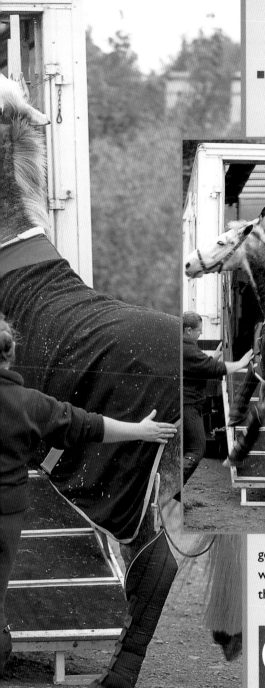

movement. Your job is to keep your horse's mind on the task in hand and to reward him for every little try.

- Let your horse paw or sniff the ramp – this is perfectly natural behaviour as the wild horse within him is telling him to check that it is safe to put his feet on the ramp. When your horse tries to convince himself that all is well, give him a rub on the head to tell him he's good.

- When he gets distracted and does not try, redirect his attention so that he is facing the ramp again.

- Sometimes a horse will step onto the ramp and then back off again. Do not try to stop him; feed him enough rope so that he can move back. Once he has stopped, simply ask him to move forwards again straightaway. The horse will realise that he has to deal with the problem.

Horses usually test out all methods of escape before walking into a trailer. They will go backwards, go off one side of the ramp and then off the other side. Don't get angry when your horse does this. Simply bring him back and position him so that he can go forwards into the trailer.

Q What are the signs that a horse is boss over its owner?

On the ground, a horse who is boss will step into his handler's way and have no regard for their personal space. The horse may nip his owner's arm while he is being led or rub his head on them, often knocking them flying in the process. He will often be bargy and ill mannered when being led, and use his weight and size to push his handler off balance and back them off.

Signs that the horse is boss when he is being ridden include snatching at the reins, drifting off to grab a mouthful of grass, and evading the bit. In extreme cases the horse may even attempt to smear his rider against a wall or buck or rear to get rid of them.

hitting the helper en route. The problem is that the horse has not truly bought into the idea of going into a lorry and so every time he is asked to do so, he gets anxious, and in many people's eyes he misbehaves. All the horse is really saying is that he's not sure about this process and needs some help

DEALING WITH HIGHLY-STRUNG THOROUGHBREDS

Racehorse breeders Paul and Emma are regulars at Mike's yard to get the best start in life for their Thoroughbred youngsters.

Of all the racehorses they have bred, loved and done battle with, two horses stand out from the crowd due to their particularly eccentric ways.

Flossy: who was pronounced unbreakable

The first is two-year-old homebred Thoroughbred filly, Flossy, who was always a tricky one to handle. Born with a nervous, edgy streak, Flossy's behaviour often bordered on the extreme.

She led a life of luxury in idyllic surroundings, yet once panicked when Emma went to catch her, ramming through a post-and-rail fence and galloping full-pelt across a busy road. This utter hatred of being caught created many problems for Paul and Emma. They often had to herd her into a pen to catch her and were at a loss as to what could have caused this phobia.

Flossy's neuroticism really came to the fore when she was sent away to be broken in. The plan was for her to spend two-and-a-half months with a trainer, but she wouldn't even let him brush her, let alone put a saddle on her back. Whenever he tried to do this she literally threw herself on the floor.

When an altercation between Flossy and her trainer led to him suffering a broken hand, he understandably threw in the towel and admitted he couldn't handle the feisty little mare. She was the first horse he had ever had to give up on.

Fresh from the trainer's yard, Flossy arrived home and promptly escaped from her paddock, crashing through a wall in the process. Paul and Emma thought it best to pack Flossy off to Mike's yard to give her a final chance to redeem herself.

Mike's Solution: 'Flossy was a very nervous little horse when she arrived,' says Mike. 'She was frightened of virtually everything and wouldn't allow anyone near enough to show her how things were done. As a result, she became more and more confused by life and, in turn, more neurotic.

'Flossy spent five weeks at my place, and for the first three of those I did very little with her. I had to work on gaining her respect and trust very, very slowly. There was no rushing her: if I even tried to push her on slightly she simply stopped listening and put her defences up.

'Once I had managed to get Flossy thinking about me and what I was asking her to do, her attitude started to soften. As soon as we had reached that stage I could start introducing new things into her training. I took it slowly and tried to make friends with her and soothe her nerves, and gradually she came round.

'By the end of the third week I was riding Flossy and, after five weeks, she was going really well. She trusted me and, although she was still a little insecure, she'd cracked her nerves and was 100 per cent more confident in herself.'

A total change in behaviour

Paul and Emma were astounded at the change in their little mare. They had begun to wonder whether Flossy would ever settle down to the extent that she could be trained, and were delighted at her progress. She was great to handle, not only in the saddle but on the ground too, and the disturbing behaviour that she had previously displayed had vanished along with her nerves.

As soon as Flossy came back from Mike's she went straight into a racing yard for further training, where the lads were queuing up to ride her out as she was the quietest on the yard. She then enjoyed a summer relaxing in the fields – and didn't try to escape once – before going back into training. She is now set to enjoy a career as a National Hunt racehorse, and her neurotic tendencies are a thing of the past.

Milly: too confident for her own good

The second hot-headed mare which Paul and Emma had trouble dealing with was cheeky youngster, Milly. Life dealt the little filly a cruel blow as her mum died when she was just eight weeks old. As a result of this, Milly received a lot of human attention and was turned out with two ponies for company, who also indulged her. However, all this tender loving care backfired on Milly's handlers who soon found they had an over-confident, spoilt filly on their hands.

Her mum never disciplined Milly, as she was very ill while Milly was a foal, and the two ponies she lived with had never ticked her off. As a consequence, Milly started to become more and more dominant and bolshy in her behaviour.

Milly's attitude to life was simple: she knew best and everyone else had to do what she said. She was ill-mannered and bargy and totally refused to let anyone pick her feet out. Before long, Milly's behaviour had deteriorated to the point where it took four people to hold her feet up for the farrier. She was very aggressive and, as she grew, her problems got worse – which is where Mike came in.

'Milly was a really tough character to handle,' says Mike. 'We learned that her dad had been a devil to handle too, so it was obviously in her genes!'

Mike's Solution: 'I went to Paul and Emma's yard for a morning and worked with Milly, trying to get her used to having her hooves handled. Once I had managed to get through to her and communicate what I wanted, she started to co-operate. But when I showed Paul what to do, and he tried to pick her feet up, she shoved him into a wall.

'When I visited Milly a second time we worked with her again and this time Paul managed to handle her feet. She was a lot better behaved after this second session and her attitude had improved immensely.'

The turning point came when the farrier – who had previously refused to shoe Milly – managed to shoe her without any problems. He was amazed at her change in attitude and, since then, Milly has shown everyone a lot more respect. Thanks to Mike's work she is now a reformed character and a much-loved member of the yard – as opposed to a much-feared one!

7 The way forward

Think Equus offers riders and trainers a way to get the best out of their horses, one which works in all kinds of circumstances and with all kinds of horses – even with those that have shut down or have really negative attitudes to people. However, Think Equus does require the trainer or rider to use their head and work in the present moment, anticipating the horse's reactions second by second. Getting into the correct frame of mind to work with your horse can be difficult. We are all so emotionally attached to horses – even if it's a negative emotion. However, once you have managed to detach yourself for a time and coolly deal with the problem you will be on such a high!

Do not try to run before you can walk. Apply Think Equus principles to your own progress and make sure you set yourself up for success. Before you try anything else, work on the exercise to get a horse's respect and attention described at the start of this book. This exercise really is a useful key to your horse, and once you have this properly established you have a good base from which to progress.

Just as you would work within your horse's limitations so you must realise your own boundaries. Always be aware that horses are big, unpredictable creatures. Over time you will learn to read a horse's body language and to anticipate the next move – but if you are new to horse owning don't think that you can learn everything in a short time. By handling horses you will learn – but you have to think safety first. You can always take advantage of one of Mike's courses if you want an intensive session on understanding your horse.

Every horse is an individual; and, as we know from the middle ground principle, some horses are much more tolerant than others. To build your confidence and handling skills you initially need to work with generous horses, not problem horses. The latter require delicate expert handling, so do not be tempted to try to prove yourself by tackling a problem that you cannot hope to solve.

Remember that in Think Equus the goal is a target, but is not something that has to be reached at any cost. Sometimes, as you progress towards your goal, you will find that something has changed and consequently the goal has altered a little. You need to be flexible in your outlook and thinking in order to adapt to circumstances.

There is always a great temptation to throw yourself into something before thinking through the consequences – be aware of this and make sure you prepare yourself mentally before even going near your horse. Think through the problem, consider what may have caused the behaviour and how your horse might react, have a plan in your head so that you know what action to take if he does x, y or z. It is a well-known sports psychology technique to rehearse a performance in your head. This mental preparation includes how to deal with setbacks – but, of course, you also always rehearse positive outcomes.

As part of this philosophy you give your horse time to work out what he has to do – and if he is not using that time productively you remind him to get on with the job in hand. You can apply the same principle to yourself – and if something you are doing is not working then stop, review matters and try something else, always working within the boundaries of courtesy, respect, attention and commitment.

Learning to think like a horse is often exciting, occasionally frustrating, but always immensely rewarding. All horses enjoy being handled by someone who has learnt to Think Equus – for at long last horse and rider are communicating in a language that both understand.

Left: Horses have to learn to compromise in order to live happily in our world. The Think Equus philosophy enables riders and trainers to help horses adapt with as little stress as possible

Right: Horses will happily follow the lead of another horse if they are anxious about anything. Think Equus will help you become someone your horse can trust and turn to for help

SUPPORT TEAMS

One of the elements of the Think Equus philosophy is an awareness of each other – the horse being aware of you, and you being aware of the horse. We can also add to this an awareness of other people and how they can assist you both. Mike's philosophy takes a holistic view of the horse that considers all the factors that could be contributing to his behaviour or way of life. This inevitably means that at times you will need to consult other experts: vets, farriers, dentists, saddle fitters, nutritionists and instructors, and various complementary therapists.

In an ideal world you will enlist the help of someone who is experienced and well qualified, and who takes a sympathetic view of the horse. The very fact that there are so many horses with various problems shows that, sadly, this is not always the case.

WHAT CAN YOU DO TO ENSURE THAT THE PEOPLE YOU CONSULT ARE GOING TO WORK IN YOUR HORSE'S BEST INTERESTS?

- Check their qualifications – this is easy enough with people like vets and farriers, but what about other therapists? Do question people: don't just take their word. Ask about their training, the type and timescale. A reputable person will be happy to prove that he or she is a member of a professional body, has qualifications, adheres to a code of conduct, has the relevant insurance and so on. Do be aware that some people go on a weekend course and then set themselves up as experts in a particular field. Be very careful about who you allow to become involved with your horse!
- If planning to use therapists, such as chiropractors or physiotherapists, ask your vet to recommend someone. Be aware that some vets have an enlightened attitude towards other therapies, but others do not. The attitude of the therapist towards the vet is also important – they should not be treating your horse unless they have the vet's permission. Some therapies – Equine Muscle Release Therapy is an example – are relatively new, and not all vets are yet aware of them. However, no EMRT practitioner would treat a horse without first having the vet's permission.

Equine Muscle Release Therapy is a gentle yet effective therapy, and is especially helpful for horses with soft tissue problems

- Look for professional listings. This at least confirms that the instructor has reached a certain standard, has training in first aid and is insured. All professional bodies hold lists of their members.
- Try to find word-of-mouth recommendation for dentists, therapists, instructors and trainers. If you are new to an area, ask the 'expert' whose help you are considering to give you the names of other clients you could speak to.
- Question your expert before committing yourself. Find out about costs, frequency of visits, back-up service and so on.
- If your vet is prescribing drugs for your horse you have a right to know what they are and what they are expected to do. A vet can explain all this. So, if you are asking a complementary therapist for help, can they also tell you about the oils or potions or remedies they are using, their effects, any adverse side effects and so on? A properly trained person will be able to; on the other hand, someone who has just completed a day's course and thinks they know it all could be very dangerous! Don't be fooled into thinking that because something is natural it is safe – Mother Nature has lots of poisons in her repertoire!
- Trust your own instincts – if someone makes you feel uneasy, walk away. You are asking for help with a trusted friend, your horse, so you have to be comfortable with the person you are 'employing'.

Complementary therapies are now being used for animals, some with good result

Fortunately there are masses of cases where people have worked together to improve a horse's life. This practice of co-operation between the various branches of equine expertise is growing, and can only help as we all try to Think Equus and enjoy better relationships with our horses.

CASE STUDY

HELPING CANDY

A few years ago co-author Lesley had a very frustrating time with her mare Candy. As the horse's fitness programme progressed they always seemed to reach a point at which the mare became unlevel. The problem was subtle and one that Lesley could feel, although even her instructor could not spot that Candy was not 100 per cent sound. A vet was consulted; he could see the problem but investigations did not reveal any cause. The mare had some time off, was brought back up, reshod and started work again. Once again, as the work progressed the problem resurfaced. At the same time Lesley's farrier commented that Candy was wearing down one heel more than the other and he could not work out why. He and Lesley decided to get together with the vet to try to sort things out. All three met at the veterinary surgery and were able to enlist the help of the visiting physiotherapist too.

As a result they pieced together a jigsaw puzzle and resolved the issue! The physio found a slight difference in the mare's muscles on the hind leg diagonally opposite the front foot that had the heel problem. The other hind leg had an old injury. At the time of the injury a vet examined the mare but it was not immediately realised that she had fractured a splint bone. As a result she spent a few days moving slightly differently in order to compensate for the injury, putting more strain on the 'good' hind leg. Over time, this very slight change in her movement affected the diagonally opposite front limb, causing the heel to wear down. The farrier shod the mare differently behind to encourage correct movement, the heel stopped wearing down and the mare was no longer unlevel.

Each person involved held a piece of the jigsaw, but without the input of the others the information made no sense. As an instructor and EMRT practitioner Lesley promotes the idea of specialists working together to help horses and has so far worked successfully with vets, dentists, physiotherapists, saddle fitters and trainers to help horses overcome various problems.

A holistic approach was needed in order to get to the bottom of this mare's soundness problem

Appendices

Michael Peace and Think Equus

If you would like to find out more about Think Equus, Michael Peace offers private lessons, group clinics and holds lecture demonstrations throughout Britain and abroad. It is also possible to send horses for schooling at his Oxfordshire base.

Private consultations

Michael will come to visit you and your horse wherever you are and work on any area of your horsemanship that you wish to improve. This is a popular and effective way of tackling issues with loading, shoeing and clipping, or solving schooling problems.

Send your horse for schooling

Whether you want your horse started correctly, ridden for the first time, made easier to handle, better to load, easier to clip, better to shoe or his/her ridden work improved, you can send your horse for a week or two for schooling by Michael at his Oxfordshire base.

Group clinics

If you want to get a group together who would like to learn more about Think Equus, you can arrange for a visit from Michael for either a half or full day of tuition. Group clinics, which can include spectators as well as riders, are excellent for riding clubs, college students pony clubs and small private stables and can be tailored to suit the group's requirements.

Business seminars

For a fresh approach to management training, Michael is available to demonstrate how the Think Equus philosophy has valuable business applications.

Book and video

Michael's first book, *Think Like Your Horse*, and his video of the same name can be purchased from his website.

Contact Michael at PO Box 230, Kidlington, Oxfordshire, OX5 2TU. Tel/fax 01865 842806. Email: michael@thinkequus.com Website: www.thinkequus.com

Lesley Bayley

Equestrian consultant and specialist Lesley Bayley offers freelance instruction in both riding and horse care. She takes a holistic approach to horse and rider, using both traditional and alternative methods, tailored to suit the needs of the individual. Lesley is an Equine Muscle Release Therapy practitioner and is based in Leicestershire.

Contact her on 01572 787257
Email:lesley.bayley@virgin.net

Equine Muscle Release Therapy

EMRT is a very gentle, non-invasive therapy, adapted from the Bowen technique that is practised on humans and taught all over the world. The therapy works on the muscle and soft tissue fascia at specific neuro-muscular trigger points of the body. It activates the horse's own healing mechanisms to release muscle spasms, address skeletal im-balances and increase blood supply to the affected areas. It also increases lymphatic drainage so that dysfunction debris, which interferes with healthy muscle and joint activity, is cleared away.

Treatments are carried out with a vet's permission and take approximately 45 minutes. EMRT was developed by Alison Goward in Australia, and the FEI allow the therapy to be used on the day of competition.

For details of accredited EMRT practitioners in the UK contact Sue Connolly on 01789 772413. To contact the Australian office email emrt@ozemail.com.au

Neuro Linguistic Programming

NLP is a way of thinking, and a collection of very effective techniques, which can help riders in all aspects of their lives. NLP examines the mind and how we think, the language we use and how it affects us and other people, and how we act to achieve our goals. As a rider, NLP can help you to overcome nerves, clarify your ambitions, improve your communication techniques with your horse, your instructor and, if you teach, your pupils. It has endless applications to riding and is a fascinating subject. For more information read:

Introducing NLP by Joseph O'Connor and John Seymour (Thorsons)
Schooling Problems solved with NLP by Wendy Jago (J.A. Allen)
Simple Steps to Riding Success by Liz Morrison (David & Charles)

Useful contacts
Equine dentistry
BEVA
020 7610 6080

Farriery
Farriers Registration Council
01733 319911
www.farrier-reg.gov.uk

Index

Acknowledgments

I would like to dedicate this book to my sons Charlie and Henry for giving me a clearer perspective in life.

Also, my mum and dad for their selfless support and encouragement in the early days of my career with horses.

Thanks to Lesley and her husband Martin – without him this book might never have materialised.

Finally, to my wife Susi for being there to share my life.

Michael Peace

A DAVID & CHARLES BOOK
Copyright © David & Charles Limited 2002, 2007

David & Charles is an F+W Publications Inc. company
4700 East Galbraith Road
Cincinnati, OH 45236

First published in the UK in 2002
Reprinted 2002, 2003
First paperback edition 2007

Text and illustrations copyright © Michael Peace
and Lesley Bayley 2002, 2007

Michael Peace and Lesley Bayley have asserted
their right to be identified as author of this work in
accordance with the Copyright, Designs and Patents
Act, 1988.

Horse care and riding are not without risk, and while
the author and publishers have made every attempt
to offer accurate and reliable information to the best
of their knowledge and belief, it is presented without
any guarantee. The author and publishers therefore
disclaim any liability incurred in connection with
using the information contained in this book.

A catalogue record for this book is available from
the British Library.

ISBN-13: 978-0-7153-1297-1 hardback
ISBN-10: 0-7153-1297-9 hardback

ISBN-13: 978-0-7153-2691-6 paperback
ISBN-10: 0-7153-2691-0 paperback

Printed in Singapore by KHL
for David & Charles
Brunel House   Newton Abbot   Devon

Commissioning Editor Jane Trollope
Desk Editor T F McCann
Art Editor Sue Cleave
Project Editor Sue Vicars
Production Controller Adrian Buckley
Photographer Bob Atkins

Visit our website at www.davidandcharles.co.uk

David & Charles books are available from all good
bookshops; alternatively you can contact our Orderline
on 0870 9908222 or write to us at FREEPOST EX2
110, D&C Direct, Newton Abbot, TQ12 4ZZ (no stamp
required UK only); US customers call 800-289-0963 and
Canadian customers call 800-840-5220.